SEVENTY TIMES SEVEN

76694

SEVENTY TIMES SEVEN

Robert Hoyer

Nashville
Abingdon

Seventy Times Seven

Copyright 1976 © by Robert Hoyer

All rights in this book are reserved.
No part of the book may be reproduced in any manner whatsoever without written permission of the publishers except brief quotations embodied in critical articles or reviews. For information address Abingdon Press, Nashville, Tennessee.

Library of Congress Cataloging in Publication Data

HOYER, ROBERT.
  Seventy times seven.
  1. Christian life—Lutheran authors. I. Title.
BV4501.2.H645   248'.48'41   75-30668

ISBN 0-687-38199-1

MANUFACTURED BY THE PARTHENON PRESS AT
NASHVILLE, TENNESSEE, UNITED STATES OF AMERICA

CONTENTS

Introduction 7
Synopsis 9
The Story Continued 19
An Act of Faith 21
Freedom to Forgive 24
A Poor Miserable Sinner 30
Justly Deserved 35
The First Stone 40
He Did It Again 48
All Sorts and Conditions of Sin 54
As We Forgive Our Debtors 62
A Good or Bad Reputation 69
Not Ashamed 76
The Sheep and the Goats 86
The Yoke of Falsehood 92
Capital Forgiveness 97
Epilogue: Happily Ever After 106

Introduction

The kingdom of heaven is like a high school class with all sorts and conditions of students. There are the rich and the poor, the smart and the stupid, the diligent and the lazy, the white and the black. The teacher gave the class a test, examined the results, and announced: "Look. You have all flunked the course. There is no possibility that any of you can do anything to earn a passing grade. But here is what I will do. I will leave the room, and you can give one another passing grades. Whomever you pass I will pass, and whoever will not pass everyone else I will flunk."

The teacher left and the argument began. The diligent did not think the lazy deserved a passing grade. The smart ones did not want to be listed as equal to the stupid. The rich passed one another and ignored the poor. The white students said that each race should do its own passing, but the lines should not be crossed. In each separate conflict the lazy and the stupid and the poor and the black said that under the circumstances they could not pass anyone who would not pass them.

They began to organize. Soon there were a dozen groups, each with its formal rules on how to pass. Each group claimed that its rules were the only valid ones. They entered happily into the conflict. They wrote long papers justifying

SEVENTY TIMES SEVEN

their positions and organized rituals of group identity. It even occurred to some that the only way to achieve a passing grade was to eliminate everyone who disagreed.

Until one student remembered the words of the teacher. He stood up and said, "We have all already flunked. I want to pass. I have decided to pass everybody without any distinctions at all." Some who heard him gathered around him, the happy fellowship of those who knew that they would pass. They joined the groups—any group. They observed the rituals, they kept the rules. But they trusted none of it. They knew that there was no salvation from flunking out except in the simple promise of the teacher.

When the teacher returns to the classroom, to whom will he give a diploma?

Synopsis

The story in this book is what you are doing to create the world you live in. The preceding chapters are all that has happened until now—all the words of God and men. This synopsis is to lead you into the story.

The beginning is God creating the heavens and the earth. All order in that creation, after the primal chaos of simple being, is established in words. God said, "Let there be light," and there was light. He said, "Let the waters be gathered . . . and the dry land appear." And it was so. He made man and woman in his image—conversable with him—and he said, "Let them have dominion." And it was so. Since then, the words by which our world is ordered to be what it is have been spoken by the people God has made.

It is a world of Tyrannosaurus Rex and the rabbit, a world with both the ant and the redwood tree, the weak and the strong. When God saw everything that he had made, he called it very good. He gave it to us as a garden. He places each of us in that garden with his blessing.

He designated two trees in that garden as special: the Tree of Life and the Tree of the Knowledge of Good and Evil. The names are significant. The Tree of Life is the tree of grace, as God saw what he had made. The Tree of the Knowledge of Good and Evil is the tree of law, the words which distinguish between the good act and the evil act, between the good man and the evil man.

SEVENTY TIMES SEVEN

God has warned us in the garden, "Do not eat of that second tree. On the day you choose it you will surely die. Do not make the distinctions, do not order your world and relate to one another in the words of good and evil. That is the way of death."

We chose the Tree of the Knowledge of Good and Evil. It seemed good to us, and the logical way to maintain order in the garden. That choice is our original sin, the sin out of which all enmity and lust and competition and fear have grown. All the way back to the beginning of our talking together in words, we have structured our world in the knowledge of good and evil, and the world we have made is not a garden.

We have lost grace. No one has a hope of knowing himself as good except in contrast to someone else's evil. We are conscious of no right to be unless we can deny that right to someone else. We have even made God in our image, picturing him as one who condemns the evil man and blesses the good. It is not surprising that when we made the choice we were afraid. We hid ourselves from God. Because in our choice we have never known just where he is, we have been diligently hiding from one another. In the words of the knowledge of good and evil, no one can afford to be known.

God, whose grace can call the virus and the saber-toothed tiger good, found us. He has judged us: there is no difference between us. We have all failed. It is not a judgment of law, it is a word of grace. There is hope in the judgment if only we can speak the words to one another and create our world around them. So God judged us and gave us hope.

The hope has been there from the beginning. It is the

SYNOPSIS

reason for the calling of Israel, the sealing of their covenant, the words of their prophets, and the events of their history. But we could not hear the hope clearly in our own world of the words of law. We made distinctions and separations out of the words of hope. We erected temples and high places to our own purity. We stoned and starved the prophets who came to correct us. We chose the Tree of the Knowledge of Good and Evil, and the garden is lost. There is no way back to the tree of grace until we die to the world of law that we have created.

God has found us, and he will not let us go. We killed the prophets that he sent, but in the proper time he sent us one to whom we must listen. Jesus of Nazareth called us through the death of our pride into the kingdom of heaven.

The Word Was Made Flesh

The kingdom of heaven is about a man talking. He was born into a world of heated conflicting words, and he changed it. "Look," he said, "I make everything new." The kingdoms of this world have become in his words the kingdom of our God and his Christ. To those who believe, he gives power to become the sons of God, heirs of the kingdom. It is the power of words. He said, "If you continue in my word you will know the truth, and the truth will make you free." He wasn't talking about spiritual freedom or inner peace. He meant freedom from Rome and the Pentagon, freedom from robbers on the road and crime in the streets, freedom from the ubiquitous tax collector, freedom from the fears of fate and rejection and loneliness. Name the power that threatens you: his words have conquered it. Now the words are yours.

SEVENTY TIMES SEVEN

Three hundred years before Christ was born, Alexander the Great tried to unite the world with words. They were Greek words of politics and drama, athletic games and philosophy. When Jesus was born, there were still many who believed that if everyone would adopt the language of reason there would be peace. One hundred years before Jesus was born, the Romans stepped in and tried to unite the world with trade, the words of commerce. There were many who believed that if everyone would do his job and support the process there would be prosperity.

There were also more limited local words. In Jerusalem some talked about righteousness and the covenant of God and keeping the ancient law. They believed that God would give his people power and influence to lead the world into glory—if they were faithful to their calling. Some others wanted to force God's hand. They talked of rebellion and the destruction of Roman power. Another group said there was no hope. They went out into the desert and talked about waiting for God to send his own deliverer with words of salvation.

Jesus was a middle-aged rabbi who came into these confused worlds of words and began to preach. He used all the familiar words, but the way he used them created a different world. The people flocked to hear him, fascinated. He told stories. They were simple stories out of the common experience, but they had sudden twists that turned the old worlds around.

All the people knew what "kingdom" meant. A king held power over a country with an army. He made laws to control the people. He fought to protect them from their enemy. They supported him and obeyed him to keep the peace. But Jesus talked about a kingdom of heaven. He

SYNOPSIS

never mentioned a king or an army or power or laws or fighting. The kingdom grows between men like yeast in a lump of dough. No one has any authority over anyone else there. Like a field with both wheat and weeds growing together, no one controls anyone else. The kingdom is so great that a man will sell all he has to get it, but it is not in any particular place that you can go. The people do not pay taxes or support their king; they are supported and are free to use the bounty that is given them.

The people who heard the words wanted a place in the kingdom, so they fought to deserve it and argued which of them would be the greatest. They all knew what greatness meant: power, fame, authority. Jesus called a little child and set him in the circle. He said, "That's greatness. Be like a child. If you want to be great in the kingdom, be a servant, a slave." Greatness comes by giving, not by getting.

They all knew what "righteousness" meant. They had the laws and the volumes of interpretation. They had models, the Pharisees, who were good honorable men, just and fair and law-abiding. Jesus said, "That's not enough. Don't trust it." He imitated Moses on the mountain and recast the ancient laws, saying in effect, "Do not pretend that you have kept a law. You haven't." He said to one of the Pharisees, "You must be born again." You have to start over a different way. It is by mercy and not by performance that a person is righteous.

People had their fantasies about the good life then just as they have now: freedom, wealth, popularity, health, a long life. Jesus reversed them all: "Continue in my word, the truth will make you free. Do not be anxious about food and drink and shelter, they are secondary. You have the kingdom, and you can afford to give everything else away." They brought to him a man so sick his friends had to carry him, and Jesus said, "Son, be happy. Your sins are forgiven." He said, "Whoever tries to save his life will lose it. Whoever loses his life for me and for the kingdom will save it. The poor are the happy ones, and those who mourn, and the meek, the merciful, the peacemakers, and those who are persecuted for their mercy."

Jesus took his people's sacred traditions and reshaped them in his own way. They wanted him to keep the Sabbath because, they said, God has rested on the seventh day at creation. Jesus did his work of healing and said, "The Sabbath rules are there for the sake of men. My Father never stopped working. He is still creating." He sat with his disciples at the Passover meal, for more than a thousand years the festival of independence and freedom. He took the symbols of the old covenant and said, "After this, when you eat and drink together do it to remember me."

He made a world with his words. It was a new world, completely strange to us who had eaten of the Tree of the Knowledge of Good and Evil. His cousin John, who had been sent to announce his coming, was perplexed. He sent a committee to ask Jesus, "Are you the one we expect, or is someone else coming?" Jesus answered, "Watch what I do, listen to what I say, go back and tell John that the man is happy who does not wish I were something else." His disciples told him, "These are hard words. Who can hear them?" Jesus asked, "Do you want to leave?" Peter said, "To whom could we go? You have the words of eternal life."

He did not promise that the kingdom was coming, nor did he set down any conditions for us to meet first. He said it is here between us. We have it when we live and talk together

SYNOPSIS

as though it were here between us. As Jesus lived. His friends were from every condition of life: Pharisees and publicans, prostitutes and priests, laborers and dreamers. They all learned from him the one rule of the kingdom: that we love one another as he loved us.

We couldn't take it. He refused to condemn the traitors who worked for Rome, he would not even reject the Romans who had subdued us. He did not bless the good people because they were good, and he never condemned the evil people for their evil. He condemned only those who felt it their right to judge others. Well, we had our pride. Each of us knew in what way he was good. Each of us knew other people who were worse. Jesus would not accept our way. He refused to give us credit for being right, and he would not let us show that someone else was wrong.

In the last week he forced us to choose between our own self-justification and his grace. We chose again the Tree of the Knowledge of Good and Evil. We condemned him as a danger to all that we held sacred, a blasphemer who presumed to speak for God. We took him out and killed him, laying on him the iniquity of our fears, hates, and lusts.

He rose again from the dead and sent his disciples out with power to beseech us, "Be reconciled to God—die to your pride and live in grace together." Their plea has passed from generation to generation, the plea to image God as grace in Jesus Christ. To those who follow him, who die with him to the law that draws distinctions between us, he gives power to become the sons of God.

The Battle for Survival

We are still fighting against the words of Jesus. We do not want to die. We try to escape his world. We are not comfortable in it, we do not fully trust him. Through the centuries we have tried again and again to create proud worlds, with just enough of his words to claim that our worlds are his.

We made worlds of doctrine and ritual. We said God was wrathful and just, that he could not forgive until his wrath was satisfied. Jesus, we said, was the sufficient sacrifice to reconcile God to man; but only those who believed it were counted good. We created that world on our own doctrines of what Jesus did, ignoring what he said. Then in his name we sent crusades to kill the Turks, we tortured heretics to confession and hanged witches to save their souls.

In revulsion we made worlds of ethics and discipline. We said that the words of Jesus were our rule, but we talked about his commandments and his example. Somehow the rules—like any rules—were meant for other people. We used the words of Jesus to counsel contentment and obedience in poverty. We bled the weak with work and comforted the slave with the promise of heaven.

We didn't all go on the crusades. Most of us did not hang witches. Only a few of us ran sweatshops and got rich. But nearly all of us spoke the words that created the world in which crusades and witch fever and slavery happened. We spoke them because in those worlds we could be proud. We used the Turk and the witch and the slave to prove our own validity, saying, "He is not as good as I am!" We did exactly that, and we carefully taught our children to say it after us, denying the world that Jesus came to create.

Jesus told us that every person who heard his words and did them—lived in the world they create—would be like a person whose house is built on rock. Well, we heard the words, but we did not heed them. The house we built in the

SYNOPSIS

world that we created is built on sand. That house is the churches on the corners of our cities, the God-homes we go to on Sunday morning. The rain fell, the floods came, and the winds blew and beat against our house. Wherever it is built on the sand of our own righteousness, it is falling. The newspapers and the TV tube are recording its fall piece by piece.

We need the words of Jesus, creating the new world he called the kingdom of heaven. We make that kingdom come with our words, if they are his words as he used them. But that is a community project. No one has a language all by himself, words mean what a whole society of people agree on when they talk. No one can bring in the kingdom by himself. Jesus began it by gathering twelve men around him and talking.

Any person who has the words of Jesus can do the same. He can use those words and fill them with the meaning Jesus gave them. He can transmit the words and the meanings to others. He can form a community of people who speak as Jesus spoke, who continue in his words. That is the building of the kingdom, and there is no other way.

Jesus did not start a church, at least not in the sense of people who assemble on Sunday morning to hear a man preach and then gather on the sidewalk to talk about the weather and the baseball scores. Jesus called twelve men to learn his words, and he sent them out to talk. They and whoever heard and acted on his words, were to go into the assemblies of men to name the name and tell the stories of Jesus. For as long as that happened the kingdom grew like a mustard tree, like seed sown in rich soil. It will grow again when those who have heard his words return to the marketplaces to talk in his name. Wherever a few are

SEVENTY TIMES SEVEN

gathered and his words are spoken, Jesus is there, creating.

Jesus did not intend the church as we have made it. But the church is what we have to start with. It is given to us to work in, just as St. Paul was given his people's synagogues in every city where he worked. Any one of us can use the words of Jesus in his church, to form there a community that hears and does the words. If we do, the church will become again the yeast that grows to give life in the world. Then the kingdom comes as we pray it will, every Sunday when we gather together.

The Story Continued

One evening not too long ago, I was worn out with the effort of explaining to myself and to those who use my writing the relationship between God, whom we cannot know, and his church, which talks about him. I fell into the half-doze that precedes sleep, and I dreamed a vision of my place before God.

I stood as though in a small empty theater, alone. The stage on which I stood opened at the back into vast loneliness, like a deserted ocean beach on a cold night. I was standing on a wooden platform about four feet square, with a low railing. It was built of used lumber, the surfaces charred and soiled, but the edges clean and newly cut. The platform was solid and well built. Beneath it was a wooden walkway stretching to right and left. To the right there was nothing else. But to the left, fading into the distance, half a dozen other platforms stood empty. Some of them were elaborate, some very simple.

I wore a double-breasted suit, which I do not like. Two spotlights shone on me out of the theater. The rest of the scene was in twilight darkness. I turned to stage rear, and before me stretched a thick blackness which the lights could not penetrate. I felt the blackness like a heavy, vague curtain in front of me. It did not begin or end anywhere, it was just there. There was nothing else in the scene. Nothing else happened in the dream.

I knew in the vision as I watched myself on the platform that I was praying. The platforms were my postures of prayer, past and present. They were built out of the experiences of other people. They were mine, I was not ashamed of them, but nothing in the dream indicated that they were reasonable or effective. The blackness before me listened and knew that I was there, but gave no other sign. He waited. I did not feel comfortable. I could not even pretend that there was any grandeur in what I did. I was alone.

I woke and knew that this was all I would see or know of God until the vision is replaced by reality.

An Act of Faith

We do not know God. We use the word together, but we cannot share our images. The experiences which fill the word "God" with meaning are private experiences, like visions in a dream world. But ignorance is not a failure. It is a necessary part of the meaning because God is not God if he is known. The first rule given to the people of Israel at Mt. Sinai forbids the attempt to make our images evident and shareable. Whatever image we create will be false.

We who use the name of God to build a world cannot build with the same kind of surety that the physicist or the biologist have, who insist that their images must be shared in microscope or test tube before they can be counted real. Our surety is of a different, indirect order. When we pretend that our knowledge of God can be proved by logic or by touch, we err. It is our besetting sin. We construct our abstract "spiritual" worlds founded on words like "authority" and "infallibility." Then when we try to live in those worlds they turn to shadow and mist, and we are left exposed and frightened.

The error is only in the method. We are not less sure than the biologist, because his world too is created out of words shared with other people. We build the kingdom of heaven with words spoken between people, words about people and the mud and stone in which they live. The kingdom is real now between us. There is very little abstract or "spiritual" about it. It is filled with eternal hope, with praise and thanks to God, but it is created out of such common events as eating and drinking together, being born and marrying and dying, building houses and tearing them down again.

The tool with which we take these common events and their common words to make the kingdom of our Lord is called an act of faith. It is something we do, speaking the words of Jesus to one another in the doing *because* we believe his world is real and is the world we want. The act is in our everyday world of getting and spending; an act by which we deliberately mold that world with the words of Jesus into something new: the kingdom of heaven.

The primary act of faith is forgiving. It is the characteristic act of God, the Father of Jesus Christ. If we follow him in faith, it is the first thing we do in our following. It is the one different thing we do in faith which we would not do if we had no faith. It is what we start with if we want to put meaning and purpose back into our lives.

The act of forgiving involves word relationships between people. We have to talk together to forgive. It is a world-building act, like any talking. But forgiving constructs a world of faith and fellowship without fear and anxiety. It is not private like prayer or giving to the poor. It is necessarily an open public act between people, out where words do create worlds.

Forgiving is not a moral act. That is, it is not an act done in obedience to a law or a custom. No one forgives because he ought to forgive. The pressure of laws and oughtness diminishes the act of forgiving. It is an act of faith: a person forgives because he believes—that the world created in

AN ACT OF FAITH

forgiving is a happy world. I forgive, when I forgive, because I can—not because I must.

It is not easy. I do not pretend to do it well. Nor does anyone else I know. I forgive in a stumbling search for a vision I see only faintly of a world that is a beautiful garden blessed by God. I have the example of some experts who are far beyond me in their practice of grace. They are all the kind of people I would like to be, they live in a world where I would like to live. They have heard the words of Jesus, and they are following him in an act of faith.

The following means a denial of human nature, a turning away from the normal patterns of life. It is a conversion, not just of the heart but of the whole life. It is taking the clay of everyday life—clay shared by every other human—and shaping it into a new and different world. With the words of Jesus.

Your common sense will tell you that I am wrong, when I describe the way of forgiveness. By common sense, I *am* wrong. But that is the whole point. Our common sense has not made a very beautiful world for us, and there is a better way. The sense of Jesus is not common. It is the way of the Holy Spirit, calling us out of the common and into love and joy and peace.

Freedom to Forgive

Moses led God's people out of subjugation in Egypt and on the way to their own land. They remembered and recorded the covenant God made with them: the year of terror before the Exodus when plagues on the land forced the agreement with Pharaoh; the first three months of the journey when God delivered them from crisis after crisis; the coming to Sinai, a desolate rock overlooking an even more desolate valley. This was the place. For three days they prepared for the establishment of their covenant. God promised them that if they accepted and kept it, they would be his people and he would be with them.

The drama of the covenant began early on the third day. A thick cloud covered the mountain top. Thunder cracked and lightning flashed. There was the sound of a trumpet so loud that everyone trembled. They assembled at the foot of the mountain, now covered with fire and smoke. The trumpet blast grew louder.

God spoke from the mountain in the hearing of all the people. He said, "I am Yahweh, your God, who brought you out of the land of Egypt." Everyone there remembered, everyone knew that they stood there by God's decision, in God's power, under God's protection. In the face of that awesome drama no one could think that he had earned or deserved his deliverance.

FREEDOM TO FORGIVE

Then God spoke the words of covenant agreement. I have to interpret the first words, because they have become too familiar. He said, in effect, "Remember my power, my grace in delivering you. If you take my covenant and stand before me, you shall have no other kind of God. You shall never try to picture me in any way, you shall not try to imagine what I am like. You shall not take my name in vain; once you call yourselves my people I will hold you to the agreement. One day in every seven you will do no work, to remember that I have made you and called you."

The laws of interpersonal relationship followed. But the people demonstrated the human response to unanswerable law, they backed away in fear. They told Moses, "You go up and talk to him and tell us what he says. Do not let us hear that voice again, or we will die."

All human laws are in a sense the laws of God. They identify us in being, they reveal our image of what we are. They are intended to save us from the troubles of our life together, to redeem us from evil. They are administered to guide us in the way of right. These are the functions of the word "God" in any language. Human societies have always transcendentalized their laws and their mores, convinced that they reflect a power and a truth beyond the human realm.

The same thing is true also of the ancient Hebrew covenant. Yet there is a difference. The laws of every other human society distinguish between the good man and the evil man. The law formed in the Hebrew insight does not. It leaves no man innocent. At Mt. Sinai every individual person recoiled in fear, knowing himself judged.

The law of the Hebrew image of God states that there are no good men. The Christian church has reflected this

SEVENTY TIMES SEVEN

statement in its doctrine of total depravity, the universality of original sin. The church has largely ignored its own doctrine in practice and has judged men good or evil, demonstrating the truth of its doctrine: No man is ever free of the original sin, the choice of the Tree of the Knowledge of Good and Evil.

We are forced by our choice of law as a way of relationship to justify ourselves, to defend ourselves against condemnation. Under that force, every man defines what is right and good by his own personality, formed by his image of God. Since laws are made by those in power, laws always function to maintain the power structure. But the law given in the insight of the Hebrew nation is always in opposition to the power structure in every other human law. It is not a "higher law" distinguishing good men from evil by a better criterion. It is a denial of the validity of law as a way of relationship between men, as a way of salvation.

Therefore God commanded his people to form no fixed image of him. When we do, either in stone or in words, we use that image to justify our judgment of other men as good or evil. We demonstrated our ability to solidify a God-image and use it for our own proud purposes in the centuries after Sinai. Even that shattering experience became in our hands a means of justifying ourselves.

When Jesus came he found us comfortable in the law. The awe of its universal judgment had left us. We used it and the hundreds of interpretations we had made to judge one another and to exclude sinners from our fellowship. Jesus was a conservative in the true sense: he shook the present free from its petrified forms to restore the power of the past.

Early in his ministry he went up into a mountain to pray.

FREEDOM TO FORGIVE

He came down the next morning to find a crowd of followers assembled at the foot of the mountain. He gave them the Sermon on the Mount, a revised edition of the covenant. He said, in effect, "Do not think that I have come to abolish the law and the prophets. I have come to complete them. You have no hope of the kingdom of heaven unless you have a righteousness greater than that of the people who are comfortable with the law and think they are keeping it." He gave examples: "You have heard, 'You shall not kill.' But I say, 'Everyone who is angry with his brother shall be liable to judgment.' You have heard, 'You shall not commit adultery.' But I say, 'Whoever looks at a woman lustfully has already committed adultery.'"

The theme at Mt. Sinai was, "Avoid these things to show that God who lives among you is gracious." The theme of Jesus on the Mount was, "Do not pretend that you have avoided these things. You are not better than anyone else. God is gracious, and that is all." Jesus did not mean, "Stop looking at women if you want to be righteous." He meant, "Stop acting as though you were righteous in yourselves because you are not adulterers. You are saved by grace alone."

After reaffirming the law, Jesus stated again the whole purpose of the law: "Judge not, that you be not judged." Judgment is God's prerogative. He has judged all men equal, and no person among us is good enough to judge another.

The law of the Hebrew God says there are no good men. The Word that is Jesus Christ rejects no man as evil. The universal judgment and the unconditioned grace in Jesus Christ state that "good" and "evil" are irrelevant terms in relationships between men. We are saved by grace, "apart from the law." Your neighbor is saved by your grace in acceptance, with no distinctions of good and evil. You are saved by his grace in the same way. By the words we say to one another in grace, following the image of God in Jesus Christ, we create one another in grace, love, joy, and peace.

I remember using in my preaching the clichés of God's grace. He loves us; in his love he has redeemed us and forgiven us. There is no condition in that love, we do nothing to merit his grace or forgiveness. We only believe and trust him. The words are true but a little misleading. Only in later years have I realized that their meaning really lies in the second and the third persons. He loves you and them. In his love he has redeemed you and them, whoever "they" may be. There is no condition in that love, no merit or earning required. We and you and they only believe and trust forgiveness.

We do nothing to earn God's grace, nor does anyone else do anything to earn our grace. Forgiveness is never deserved. If it were, it would cease to be forgiveness. We are saved when unconditioned grace works salvation in and among us. When you trust forgiveness because I have forgiven; when they trust forgiveness because you have forgiven. That is the way the world is made and the way it functions. We are free to forgive.

We are priests to one another. A priest is a mediator of forgiving grace between God and man. He is not a legislator transmitting laws for the people. No one among us can make laws for the rest of us. He is not a king enforcing laws or a judge condemning the breaking of laws. No one among us has any authority over any one else. We are priests called to mediate grace to one another.

In effect, we are called to free one another from the

FREEDOM TO FORGIVE

burdens that inhibit and prevent loving forgiveness. We are to make forgiveness possible for one another. We create trust in forgiveness by being trustworthy in forgiveness. Every other system of ethics *commands* love. They say you must love to be acceptable. Jesus *permits* love. He says you are accepted, you can love. You may forgive. No fear or condemnation stands in your way.

Try it. At your dinner table tonight, in place of a table prayer, look at one another or hold hands around the table. Say in unison: "In the name of Jesus Christ I forgive you all your sins." It will probably feel uncomfortable because you are not used to it. You are making a private sentence into a formal public one. That is the point of the exercise. You are acknowledging together that forgiving is your function, that you have the power to do it. You are creating one another to live with God in a world of forgiving. Do it often enough to make the words easy and true.

Try it again at a business meeting or social gathering, particularly if the course of the talk is arousing your antagonism. Instead of counting to ten, say silently, "In the name of Jesus Christ I forgive you all your sins." If you do it often enough you may even be able to say the words aloud and make them true. They are creative words.

Use the words again when you are reading your newspaper or watching television. They will not noticeably change the news or the TV program, but they will change you. They are your free action in a covenant of grace, the way your happy world is made.

A Poor Miserable Sinner

A bright, sunny Sunday in early spring. A small town at a high altitude in the dry southwest. The day was made for joy, I was a visitor in the town where I had been a citizen some fifteen years ago. I went to church to give thanks and to meet old friends. It was an extraordinarily depressing experience. The few other worshipers were quiet and subdued. There was very little laughter among them. The hymns we sang were doctrinal, and we sang them at the pace and with the enthusiasm of a dirge:

> *Let us ever walk with Jesus*
> *follow His example pure,*
> *Flee the world which would deceive us*
> *and to sin our souls allure.*

  The sermon castigated the sins of the world, which were not in the church, and promised heaven to the faithful. After the worship on the church lawn, a man I had once called "friend" commented on the situation: "There aren't many of us. It's hard to keep the church up. I'd rather be outside on a day like this too. But at least we have heaven to look forward to. That's more than the rest of this city has. They'll find out."

  The most distressing part of the experience was that I said nothing to him. I couldn't disagree without challenging his whole world and whatever hope he had in it. He may even

A POOR MISERABLE SINNER

have learned his joyless hope from me and from what I had said years before.

We need to rid ourselves of the myth of the happy sinner. The myth identifies the Christian as one who does not indulge in the sinful pleasures of the world, but holds himself pure for the judgment of the last day. Then the tables will be reversed. The man who has drunk and danced his way through life will suffer in hell, and we who have lived lives dulled by denial will rejoice in heaven.

It's a beautifully satisfying thought. It's a divisive myth. It makes us important with no real effort on our part. We become righteous by *not* doing the things that make other people happy. It sets us against other people. There are literally millions that we can judge and condemn. We can set ourselves above them in our own self-esteem. We anticipate pleasure at their condemnation when we are finally vindicated in our righteous ways.

The myth is itself an expression of our original sin, relating to others in terms of good and evil. Even worse, the myth is false. The man who follows Jesus is not dull and miserable. The sinner, the wrong-doer, is not a happy man.

Jesus has called us into his own abundant life now. And there is no joy in any act or thought which is directed against another person.

The myth was born in the days when the church was poor, and its members envied the rich and the free. It was probably promoted by those who were rich and free to subdue the poor and the slaves. The poor accepted the myth when they could not break the power of the nobles or right the wrongs done against them. The myth served its purpose, but it is not true, and its effect is demonic.

SEVENTY TIMES SEVEN

The thief has already lost, in his act of stealing, more than he can ever take from his victim. His victim has lost money, but the thief has lost acceptance. He must justify his act by enmity against his victim because the myth by which we live prevents forgiveness. The liar has hurt himself in his lie more than he can hurt the man he lies about. He must justify himself in his lie with judgment and hatred of his victim. If he smiles, he knows his smile to be false and hollow. The man who drinks to excess is neither funny nor happy in his drunkenness. He is a tragic person who must justify his escape by anger against those who cannot forgive him. Even the murderer has lost more in his murder than the man whose life he has taken. He must continue to live knowing the hatred of his act and justifying it with further hatred.

In the same sense punishment does the punisher more harm than the evil punished can ever do. A person who wrongs another has lost fellowship, the only effective joy in life. The person who punishes has lost the same fellowship and any chance for it. He has even perverted his own self-image in the pride of his act, justifying his punishing with hatred and condemnation of the person he has punished.

No crime can ever damage the fabric of society as much as sending a man to prison for his crime. If a man steals from me, I have lost money. But he has become a thief. If I punish him, I proclaim that he has profited by his act, and his profit must be compensated with suffering. By punishing him I assume his world, in which he thought he would be happier if he had some of my money. I have even helped to convince his friends that there is some happiness in stealing from me. I have succumbed to the myth of the happy sinner and have created a false and unhappy world.

A POOR MISERABLE SINNER

These are extreme statements. It may well be that no state or large society of people could ever live with them. The heavy weight of words which have created our social worlds of right and wrong may be too formidable a mountain for the words of forgiveness to move. Crime must be punished to deter the crime and isolate the criminal because we have constructed a world in which stealing seems profitable. We do need protection against the subculture which can justify stealing and all other crimes because we have succumbed to the myth of the happy sinner.

But I am not bound by the world my larger society has made, particularly not if I can with others create a new world with the words of forgiveness. Just as the thief needs a subculture which justifies stealing in spite of punishment, so I can find a culture which knows that thief is not happy. We do not need to steal or lie or kill. We do not need to justify ourselves by saying we are better than those who do. We do not need to punish those caught in the unhappiness of crime. We can forgive.

The worst feature of the myth is the churchly inversion in what it promises. Because it calls the sinner happy, the righteous person should be unhappy. So the popular image of the church member is long-faced, sober, and self-denying, a person proud in his misery. He defines temptation as the desire for happiness and feels guilty about his own pleasure.

We have begun to realize the fallacy in our words. But the myth is so strong among us that those who want to reject the misery and the guilt feel they must reject also the society of the church. This was most strongly emphasized to me one Sunday morning while I was enjoying the fellowship of some young people in the church basement. Through our laughter we heard the worshipers upstairs, dolefully and ponderously singing: "Restore unto me the joy of thy salvation."

It is not enough for us to reject the myth and the society that sustains it. We need to construct a whole new world, with all its words and myths consistent. I can pity the man who steals from me for all that he has lost. I can sympathize with the man who lies about me or injures me for the loss he has sustained. I can do this if I have a society of friends who support me in the construction of such a world, who talk with me about the world of forgiving grace. That is what we have been called to do, in Jesus Christ. That is why we have assemblies of Christians, why we meet to talk together. We can forgive, in sympathy with the sinner, if and when we speak forgiveness to one another.

Try it. Write out on a slip of paper the name of a person whom you have been unable to forgive. Even if his "sin" is nothing more than an aggravating character trait. Put the paper in your billfold or your purse where you will notice it occasionally. When you notice the name there, think about your relationship. Do you envy the person? Would you like to be what he is? Is he happy with you as his enemy? Would he be better off if you accepted him? Use the exercise to think the reconstruction of a world.

Or try another pattern. The next time you are in a group that begins to condemn some political or church leader for his acts, take time out to try to understand his reasons, his purposes. Then talk in defense of the man. By your words try to sympathize with him and try to lead others to the same sympathy. It may not work right away. It may take a lot of practice. It will create joy. Forgiveness does work.

Justly Deserved

In the dawning years of the human race, Adam and Eve bore two sons. The older was Cain. He became a farmer, raising crops. The younger was Abel, who became a shepherd tending a flock.

Each of them brought an offering as sacrifice to God. Cain brought a sheaf of grain, and Abel brought a lamb. We are told that "God had regard for Abel and his offering, but for Cain and his offering he had no regard." We are not told how that regard was indicated. Perhaps a drought or a blight ruined Cain's crops while Abel's flock prospered.

Cain would then say that God had done this. He would have the distinct impression that his offering was not received. In the function of language, it would be enough for Cain to tell himself and anyone who would listen that his offering was not accepted, and it would be true. We make the world in which we live. Whatever the regard of God was and however it was indicated to Cain, he was angry at his brother for the acceptance he received.

So God, our God of grace who governs all our various worlds, spoke to Cain. He said, as I hear the words, "Why are you angry? Forgive your brother Abel, or you will be caught in dire evil." There was no word of accusation, no explanation of any evil that had caused the difference. God does not look to the past. There was only warning given in grace about the future.

Cain did not forgive his brother. He invited Abel out to see his crops, and there "rose up against his brother . . . and killed him."

God spoke again to Cain, asking where his brother Abel was. Cain, who could not forgive, could not accept forgiveness. He justified himself: "Am I my brother's keeper?" And at that point his evil began. God banished him from his crops and sent him out as a wandering nomad on the earth.

Cain was afraid. The punishment was more than he could bear. He said, "I will be a fugitive hated by men, and whoever finds me will kill me." So God, our God of grace, put a mark on Cain to protect him from the vengeance of men. He promised that if anyone violated the mark to punish Cain, God would exact vengeance sevenfold.

Surely, if anyone deserved punishment it was Cain. He killed his brother, even though Abel had done nothing against him and even though he had been warned by God. We could not permit such jealous rage to roam our streets. We would have to restrain it, purge it out, punish it. That is the instant human response to evil, and Cain knew it. We evaluate one another in terms of good and evil, and we punish the evildoer to disavow the evil. But the response is the response of our original sin. It is the denial of grace. So God acted in grace to protect the sinner and to prohibit our punishment. We do not need to punish. We can forgive.

It is not hard to understand why God stood between Cain the sinner and the avenger of his deed. What makes a sin sinful is that it is turned against someone else. Vengeance and punishment are exactly that, turned against the sinner.

JUSTLY DESERVED

When we punish or take vengeance we only extend and multiply the sin. We take part in the division caused by the sin. Crime and punishment are both on the same side of the human ledger, and God stands opposed to both. He stands between the sinner and the avenger *for the sake of the avenger,* to warn him away from danger just as he warned Cain. It is for our sake that he restrains us from punishing.

The statement that a sinner deserves punishment creates a world without Jesus Christ. We have created that world with great diligence for centuries. We have multiplied the laws and increased the punishments, and when men have responded in desperation with greater crime we have cried out for greater vengeance. The church, forgetting its convenant, has fulfilled its social function of legitimizing the government and transcendentalizing its rules. It has been a leader in the demand for punishment.

We pretend that we are on the side of Abel, the innocent. When God asks us gently "Where is your brother Cain?" we answer, "He is evil. We have placed him in prison, we have hanged him by the neck until he died, we have confined him in the ghetto, we cannot let him live with us."

God has avenged him sevenfold. Our world has fallen apart, torn by crime and punishment. We are afraid of one another, we walk the streets alone, we look at one another in suspicion to detect the signs of evil. We demand our rights and glare in anger when they are not given to us. There is no place for us to go in grace when the church forgets its covenant of forgiveness. And God asks us as he asked Cain: "Why are you angry? Forgive your brother, or you will be caught in dire evil."

We cannot say that the sinner deserves punishment if we take the universal judgment of God seriously. His law does not distinguish between the evil man and the good man. God builds no prison walls; he does not construct highways around the ghetto to separate man from man. No one among us can stand apart from sin to decide that someone else needs punishment. We cannot even do that as a body of good people. The statement about deserving punishment looks back at the sin, and we are caught in it. Our covenant of grace calls us to look forward to solution. In grace we cannot ask, "What is deserved?" We can only ask, "What will restore our broken unity and reconcile us again?"

In the grace of Jesus Christ we are not looking for rules about what we must do. We are rather looking for the reconciling actions we *can* do. Jesus, in his restatement of the covenant, the Sermon on the Mount, made obsolete the principle of punishment for sin. He said we do not even need to defend ourselves against evil: "If anyone strikes you on the right cheek, turn to him the other also."

We have no need to punish sin. We can forgive in order to restore relationships. We do not need to extend and multiply the sin. We do not even need to isolate the sinner to protect ourselves or break off relationship with him. We are one with him under the same judgment. We can undertake the act of reconciliation with all men and with each individual person: the act of forgiving. We can make a world without the divisive concept of punishment, a world of forgiving grace.

Try it. I will propose a hypothetical situation; you look for the next similar event in your home when you can practice the principle. Suppose that your child, in a fit of anger, breaks a lamp in your family room. You may do one of two things: Punish him for it, or sympathize with him in

JUSTLY DESERVED

the family's loss of a lamp and help him restore it or clean it up.

Punishing him will not accomplish anything good. It will only help him justify his act of anger by widening the separation between you. The only restraining force in punishment is the fear of power, and there is no love or unity in that fear. But sympathy at the loss of a lamp is a reconciling act. It is the power of forgiveness. It brings you together, and the force of love can work to restrain the next fit of anger from breaking another lamp.

Do not expect a miracle. Remember that you are working against human nature (both yours and your child's) and the words of an entire society. You may have to repeat the act of reconciliation in patient grace many times before you have recreated a world. But you can. It will work.

The First Stone

One day Jesus was sitting in the temple courtyard talking to a crowd of people. Some Pharisees brought to him a woman who, they said, had been caught in the act of adultery. They pointed out that their law, from Moses, commanded them to stone such a woman. They asked Jesus what he thought should be done with her.

The story is simple enough. It is well known, though it may not have been part of John's original writing. The motivations in the story are a little more difficult. The woman's accusers knew that they could not carry out the sentence of stoning, even if they wanted to—which does not seem likely. The Roman law prohibited it, and Rome was the real ruler of the land. They also knew that Jesus was neither judge nor jury and that they had not in any way proved their case against the woman to him. Obviously, the person on trial was Jesus, not the woman.

The crowd listening to Jesus was the jury. He had been talking about forgiveness and forgiving. But you can't forgive an adulteress just like that. At least the jury thought that, and the Pharisees knew it. Adultery is too serious a sin against the woman's husband. But if Jesus agreed with Moses or proposed any punishment at all, he would be discredited. If he said to punish, he did not mean what he said about forgiveness.

Jesus did not answer immediately. He sat there writing

THE FIRST STONE

with his finger on the ground until they asked him again, and he was sure everyone had heard and knew what was going on. Then he stood up and faced the accusers. He said simply, "Let him who is without sin among you cast the first stone." Then he sat down again and went on writing on the ground. He did not look at the woman or at her accusers.

That took courage. He had technically agreed that the woman should be stoned to death. He had instructed her accusers to get it done. He made sure that everyone there knew exactly what he had done. Then he turned his back on the whole affair, confident that nothing would happen.

The accusers melted away one by one. When only the woman was left between Jesus and the crowd, Jesus asked her, "Where are they? Hasn't anyone condemned you?" She answered, "No one, Lord." And Jesus said, "Neither do I condemn you. Go, and do not sin again."

The words of Jesus, the good news he represents, are not against the law. Note that Jesus did not try to excuse the woman or find some loophole in the law to free her. He did not ignore the law. In fact, he asserted the law and applied it as it should be applied—to everyone there. The difference between the world men create and the world of Jesus Christ is not that men have laws and Jesus has none. The same law is in both worlds. The difference lies in what we say and do when the law has been broken.

Jesus applied the law strictly and harshly. He applied it in the only way a believer in the Hebrew God could apply it: to everyone. In the test case, the woman had broken the law. But so had everyone else. When Jesus spoke, the law of God was suddenly very clear. It does not accuse the "other person." It accuses only "me," the person who reads or hears it.

SEVENTY TIMES SEVEN

The only people condemned in the story were the accusers. They acknowledged guilt when they walked away one by one. The woman stayed to hear forgiveness, they did not. As a result she could forgive them, they could not forgive her. Those who accused kept their sins, the woman they accused lost hers.

The story is not a simple conflict between some men and a woman caught in adultery. It is not even a simple conflict between some men and Jesus. Two worlds are in contrast in the story: worlds formed by the words used. The world in which the Pharisees lived defined sin by the law. The woman in their world was a sinner because she had broken a law. But the world of Jesus defined sin in personal relationships. The sinner is the person who is against someone else. The men had acted against the woman. They gained strength in their accusation like any mob does: they constructed a world by their words, a world in which they were justified in what they did.

Jesus opposed their world with words. He turned their own law against them, creating a world in which there is no justification except in forgiveness. In his world, righteousness cannot be found in law, but only in the relationship of forgiveness. In his world, being for someone is righteousness; being against someone is sin.

The story challenges us to define sin. We have all been born and raised in the world of men, where sin is defined by law. But we have to deny that world in order to understand the world of Jesus. It is not easy to do. Jesus did not find it easy either. He said clearly that he was not discarding the law or trying to escape from it. Rather, the law is not enough for a definition of sin. It merely describes what some sins are. The Pharisees who brought the woman to

THE FIRST STONE

Jesus chose the area of sexual expression for their test. For them as for us it was an area of great anxiety. If we are to deny their world and understand Jesus, we need to use their test case.

Sexual expression is not sin unless it is against someone, even when it is a breaking of the law. That is not an extreme statement, because when it is a breaking of the law it is probably done against someone. But it is the "againstness" and not the breaking alone that separates us from God and grace. The same "againstness" in sexual expression will separate us from God and grace also when it is done within the law. If we follow our sexual instincts against someone else, either physically or mentally, it is sin even though it is within the structures that the world of men has approved. The definition includes everything from the use of a prostitute with contempt through inconsiderate marital relationships to legal and financial discrimination against women.

Then the feeling that you are a better person because you have not broken the law is just as surely a sin as breaking the law. Illicit sex does not in itself separate us from God, but the thought that you are more righteous without it does. Just as telling an untruth is not a sin unless it is told against someone else, as it usually is. It is the stance against another person that makes it evil. If you feel that you are a better person because you have not told a lie, then you are against the person who has told it. In that stance against someone else you sin.

Jesus told a story about two men who went to the temple to pray. One stood and thanked God that he was not like other men—extortioners, unjust, adulterers. Then he counted his virtues—he fasted and gave 10 percent of his wealth to the poor. He was right, he did not lie. The other man prayed only, "God be merciful to me, a sinner." Jesus said the second man was justified, not the first.

No one can tell that story safely except Jesus. Every time I have tried and every time I have heard another person try, the story has been directed against someone. It is used to point out the sin of someone else, or even some other class of people. When we tell the story, we are inevitably caught in the sin of the first man: proud of ourselves because we are not like the Pharisee. But the justified person knows only his own failure.

We have chosen the Tree of the Knowledge of Good and Evil as our way of relationship to one another. We are governed by law. There is no other way open to us in the larger world of man. But the law inevitably sets us against one another. Under law we have no choice except to accuse and punish. So the law leads us into sin, without fail. It is part of our human dilemma, and we need to acknowledge it. Our very best effort at being right and our most noble hope for a world of peace—an impartial law—will always lead us further into the mire of sin and evil.

The dilemma is present also in and of the church, because the church is an organization of men. We have tried to be more righteous under law than those who are not members of the church. We have regarded it as our calling to apply the law of God more harshly and more strictly than others did. The result was inevitable. We have become more judgmental than those outside our membership. We have turned against the sinner more strongly than others have. We have condemned and punished even where the world of men has been ready to forgive. We have specifically failed in the same kind of test that the Pharisees brought to Jesus.

THE FIRST STONE

The men who brought the woman caught in the act of adultery to Jesus were asking for his response to a world of legal control. Jesus did more than escape from their clever question. He exposed the failure of legal control, of a whole legal system. His command that the man who was without sin should cast the first stone was a critical statement. He was criticizing the attitude that the law, which describes sin, requires us to condemn and punish the sinner. He said in effect that we must have another way of relating to one another. The law will fail us.

The other way is the way of forgiveness: neither do I condemn you! That other way, the other world of Jesus' words, is the true calling of the church. It is the way of the kingdom of heaven, which the church has been called to proclaim. We have not been called into being as the people of God to be more righteous under law than the world around us. We have an opposite purpose: to acknowledge our universal failure of righteousness under law and to speak to one another in the words and images of forgiveness. Our prayer is, "God, be merciful to me, a sinner."

If the people of God forget that function and speak to one another in terms of good and evil, judgment, and punishment, then we have abandoned our covenant and our purpose in the world. By our words of forgiveness we are intended to create another world to oppose and redeem the world of law. Without our creation, without the example of the kingdom of heaven in their midst, the world of men will descend step by step into conflict and enmity and fear. We are saved by grace alone, and only those who have learned from Jesus Christ to speak grace can save the world of men from destroying itself.

SEVENTY TIMES SEVEN

We can speak grace. We can forgive. The first step on the way is the acknowledgment of our own failure. The acknowledgment is not a step downward into shame. It is a step upward into grace. We do not see our own weakness with disgust, as a motivation to try harder in the world of law. We see it rather as hope, a motivation to create the other world of Jesus Christ, the kingdom of heaven where grace works.

In a court of law the judge wears a robe—in Britain even a wig—to distinguish between the office and the man. The liturgist and the preacher in a worship assembly of the church do the same thing. The theory is that the weakness and the failure of a man do not vitiate the majesty of the law or the glory of the words of grace. The robe is a mask to demonstrate the power of the law and the gospel in spite of the weakness of the man who demonstrates. But we who speak to one another in the church cannot afford such a public mask. The weakness of the officiant in the kingdom of heaven is the majesty of the law and the glory of the gospel. We can forgive only as we know our own forgiveness; we are forgiven as we forgive.

Try this. Write out the words of Jesus, "Let him who is without sin cast the first stone." Put the slip of paper into your purse or billfold. Or make a poster or banner of them and hang it in your kitchen. When you feel the need to condemn or punish someone—even your own children— remember that slip of paper or that banner. Say the words to yourself.

When that has happened several times, you will probably notice that you can become inured even to such a sentence. You will ignore it because the world of law and punishment

THE FIRST STONE

is so thoroughly in you. It is necessary for us to do more than say the words to ourselves. We are in the business of bringing in the kingdom of heaven, creating a new world. We have to say them aloud to one another.

Take a next step. When you feel the need to condemn or punish, say it positively: "I do not know what to do. I am no judge. I am no better than you. I have no right to throw stones. What can we do together to make it better for the next time?"

He Did It Again

Jesus said that if a man slaps you on one cheek, you should turn the other one. But how do you keep him from going on hitting you when you have run out of cheeks to turn? If you forgive a man for an evil act, aren't you permitting—even encouraging—him to do it again?

I told the story from John's Gospel of the woman who was caught in the act of adultery and brought to Jesus for judgment. The story ended with Jesus' words, "Neither do I condemn you. Go and do not sin again." Now use your imagination for a sequel. Suppose that the men who brought her to Jesus discovered her the next day doing the same thing. Chagrined at their defeat the day before, they brought her to Jesus again. They said, "Jesus, we know that you are a teacher who speaks for God. Your words are wise and moving. But they do not work. Yesterday you cleverly freed this woman by shaming us. But now she did it again. If you free her again, she will just repeat it tomorrow. Shall we do what Moses told us to do?"

Jesus was very clear in his statement that forgiveness never ends. He told Peter to forgive his brother "seventy times seven times." If the men brought the woman to Jesus every day for a year, with the same accusation repeated, how long do you think it would be before Jesus said, "Oh, take her out and stone her?"

HE DID IT AGAIN

The largest mountain we must move on the way to forgiveness is the fear that it will not work. Most of us have reason to doubt. We have tried a little forgiveness on our children or our friends, and they did not respond by doing what we wanted them to do. So we went back to the tested methods of control: law and punishment. That seems to work. As long as we have the power, we can control.

The concept of control is alien to the kingdom of heaven. It is a concept forced on the state by our choice of the Tree of the Knowledge of Good and Evil, and we absorb the concept with our citizenship. The state is the sum of our common choices, and it is the state's business to decide what is right or wrong, who is good or evil. But in the words of Jesus Christ we know the fallacy in the concept of control. It is never an effective deterrent to evil. Law and punishment only increase the level of evil.

Laws do not really control anyone. In a system of law the restraint is not the law itself, but the watchfulness of the law's representative. A person can do whatever he can get by with; if he has power he will do what he wants until he is checked by a greater power. Law and punishment at best only teach us to conceal and justify our evil.

When the words of law and punishment create an inhibited world with a consensus on acceptable behavior, they do achieve some control. But it is effective only in a narrow middle stratum of the society, it does not touch the powerful who are above the law or the powerless who are against the law. There is a better way.

When my children were young, they occasionally fought with one another as all children do. I followed the accepted practice, learned from kindergarten on. I tried to find out who had started the fight. I judged the guilty party,

SEVENTY TIMES SEVEN

punished him, and let the innocent party go free. It did not work, of course. It never does. The method of judging and punishing only leads a child to more determined antagonism. It teaches him not to get caught in doing wrong. It teaches him to provoke his brother into striking the first blow. It teaches him to deny guilt and to blame the other party. It teaches him to justify himself and to turn against others, to avoid punishment, and to satisfy the judge. It will not teach him the pleasure of loving his brother. The child must learn that in spite of his judge.

In the world of forgiveness, the way to deal with sin—or with whatever we regard as sin—is forgiveness. Even if a man steals from you four hundred and ninety-one times, forgiveness has not ended as the way to deal with sin. Jesus told his disciples, "If your brother sins against you seven times in a day, and turns to you seven times and says, 'I repent,' you must forgive him."

It is not clear that Jesus regarded forgiveness as a deterrent to sin. He did not propose it as a way to keep the sinner from doing it again, but it is a deterrent. In fact, it is the only effective way we have to call a man out of evil and into fellowship.

In his Sermon on the Mount, Jesus noted the difference between the world of men and his own world. The usual rule, he said, was "love your neighbor and hate your enemy." But he creates an opposite world. His rule is "love your enemies and pray for those who persecute you." Forgiveness creates a world in which there are no distinctions between "friend" and "enemy," a world where all men are under an identical relationship. In that world the deterrent is in the will and character of the citizen, not in the rules. The reason for the avoidance of evil is not

HE DID IT AGAIN

escape from punishment, but joy: "So that you may be sons of your Father who is in heaven; for he makes his sun rise on the evil and on the good, and sends rain on the just and on the unjust."

A deterrent should do more than keep a person from doing the evil that he wants to do. It should change him into one who does not want to act against others. The world of law accomplishes this only in that minority of cases where the person punished learns in addition that there is a better way to live. That learning, not the punishment, provides the deterrent to evil. Very few people can learn it from someone who stands against them. We learn it only from those who stand with and beside us. The learning is always in the forgiveness, not in the punishment.

Preventing evil is a process of education. We do have to teach our children that the world punishes to limit evil. They have to know that the law of the land has teeth: the threat of punishment. But among the people of Jesus' world we teach more: the way of grace that is contrary to the mores of the world around us. By grace we give responsibility to our youth, freeing them to fail without blame and without rejection. Every forgiveness places in their hands the freedom to respond.

We must be able to distinguish between the two worlds: the world of humanity and the kingdom of heaven. The world of humanity, which has chosen the Tree of the Knowledge of Good and Evil, is not yet able to function with forgiving grace. It is today experiencing a strong movement toward legal control through judgment and punishment. I do not understand all the psychological and sociological reasons for it, but I can see its effects in nearly every country. And I experience the tensions that it causes in the polarization of society. I realize that the church will abandon its covenant and lose its influence for good if it accompanies the world of men in the expression of judgment and punishment. We are called to be an example of the effectiveness of grace.

A little forgiveness does not work. We are not merely healers striving to minister a little medicine to an ailing world. We are followers of Jesus striving to create a new world, but we cannot create it in a little time. It would be foolish of us to propose that whole nations should operate with grace, because worlds are not made that way. They are created with the words and images of a people; the world is first created, and then the forgiveness works. If we try to use forgiveness as a deterrent outside the world made in the words and images of grace, we will fail. Then forgiveness will be a license to evil.

It does not require a whole nation to create a world. The community of the church, a group of people who talk the words of forgiveness together, can accomplish it. If we are conscious of what we are doing, and if we do it in the name of our Lord who gave us this world, we can forgive one another. We can be the example of a world of forgiveness, and we can witness to our faith by forgiving wherever we are. We may not be able to insist that others forgive, but we can do it ourselves as a confession of our faith. And we can in faith be sure that it will work.

Try it. Somewhere in your world there is a person who does not like you, who speaks against you or tries to hurt you or undermines your influence. You already know that if you retaliate in kind the problem gets worse. It deteriorates to a contest of power or popularity. Try talking to him and

HE DID IT AGAIN

about him as though he had done nothing wrong. You respect him and his motives. If he has something against you, he is alone in his antagonism. You do not share it. The act will change you almost immediately. It may in time change him. It is the only act that will.

If you have responsibility or authority that is being deliberately challenged by someone under you in the order of your world, you cannot act as though there were no problem. You can act as though the antagonism is his alone and the problem yours. Ask him what you can do about it. Talk about him with respect. It will change you almost immediately. It may in time change him. It is the only act that will.

Listen carefully to the words of those who talk about the legal control of crime. I have never met a man who said that he needed law and punishment to control himself. Those who cry out for more law and legal order want only to control the acts of others. Talk with such a person. Try to devise with him ways to govern the acts of others as he is controlled. It is by such talk that worlds are made.

Try another test. Evaluate your church or your social club. What rules of dress and decorum operate among you, whether written or unwritten? Have these rules worked to bring the sinner in to experience grace, or have they worked to keep him out? Are you enlarging your world of joy by learning to forgive, or are you making forgiveness unnecessary by trying to control?

All Sorts and Conditions of Sin

I find it hard to forgive a man who talks at great length in a meeting. He does not trust me to understand his point the first time through and leaves me no opening to ask for the one clarification that will make his case complete. I try to be patient remembering that I talk too much and tend to dominate meetings. I have probably caused exasperation more than I have suffered it. Just as I have written here with much repetition that we can forgive. But I have not defined forgiveness.

The first step in definition takes us out of the world of the words of law and punishment. Forgiveness is a word in the world of grace. We do not, technically, forgive sins. We forgive people. If I say, "I forgive you," I am not saying that you have sinned. I am saying that what you have done is now irrelevant. There is no judgment or condemnation inherent in the words of forgiveness; there is only grace in the world of Jesus Christ.

God's universal judgment that all men are sinners makes an individual's sins irrelevant. We forgive everyone for everything. A good person is forgiven for what he regards as his good in exactly the same way that an evil person is forgiven for what he knows is his evil. The only person who is not forgiven is the one who does not accept it, who

ALL SORTS AND CONDITIONS OF SIN

chooses to remain in the world of the words of law and punishment.

The formal statement, "I forgive you," may be a part of the forgiveness, but it is usually unnecessary. Forgiveness is saying in informal words and actions a whole series of things: "Yes, I know what you are and what you are doing. No, I will not join you or support you if I do not think it is wise. Yes, of course we are still friends. I think I understand why you did it or are doing it. If you want to talk about it, I will listen; if you want my opinion I will give it. But I do not insist. No, I won't tell anyone else. I don't want anyone hurt, but I know that judging and condemning hurt more than any other evil. No, I do not intend to punish you, and I will try to keep others from punishing you. Yes, of course I like your enemies. Their reasons for what they do are just as right to them as yours are to you. I will try to mend the relationships. I would like your help, but I won't insist."

I need not say all that every time I forgive. Forgiveness is first of all something that I feel toward other people, that I express by both words and actions. All the sentences that describe forgiveness show how I feel in forgiving. They are all at least implicitly in my expression to the one I forgive. Forgiveness is not just something I say to another person and then forget. It is a continuing relationship between me and him that starts with the way God feels about me and works through the way I feel about other people. It is much more like something I am than it is like something I do.

I do the forgiving not because it is a duty or because anyone is requiring me to do it. I forgive because it is a happy way to feel. When I fail to forgive, I am miserable. Failure to forgive hurts me much more than it hurts the man I do not forgive. I am forgiven, but I do not know that, nor

SEVENTY TIMES SEVEN

do I enjoy it until I forgive. God's forgiveness does not really touch me until it lives in the forgiving that I do. Forgiveness is the acceptance of people as they are; it is being happy with the way things are. It is not despair of making things any better. It is rather the only effective way of making other people better and improving all of life.

I have a friend who habitually talks too loud. It disturbs me. I have another friend who has done a magnificent job of beautifying his home. I am troubled in the same way Cain was troubled by Abel. I know another man whose apparent objective in life is to sleep with as many women as possible. Another friend is deeply concerned about correct theology. To protect that theology he has interfered in the lives of dozens of other people, some of whom are also my friends. I am probably more of a problem than any of these people, in ways I do not know. I talk too much, I am often tactless in my tendency to joke, and I am far too often sure that I am right. There is no difference, for all have sinned.

It is easy to construct a catalog of evil. We even relish doing it because we grew up with the words of good and evil. There are the violent sins of open attack on someone else. There are long-range hidden sins like overcharging for a product, cheating an employer or an employee, sexual exploitation within "the sanctified bonds of marriage," the use of half-truths and the manipulation of words when we talk about others. There are civil crimes like tyranny or graft or bribery. There are sins against public morals like pornography or drunkenness or cheating on the income tax. There are existential faults like being black or white, Jew or Gentile, beautiful or ugly, wise or stupid. And there are unnumbered little defects like nagging or being constantly late or neglecting social duty or writing books.

ALL SORTS AND CONDITIONS OF SIN

A person seldom does anything that he himself regards as evil. He may be conscious of the fact that others call it evil, but he himself has his justifying reasons for doing it. You may not agree with his reasons, but then he does not agree with yours. The sentences I have listed as the way of forgiveness apply to everyone. There is no difference. Everyone needs forgiveness. Great public crimes may seem more evil than the little faults, but the little aggravations are in the end much harder to forgive. If I want to live in a world of forgiveness, I forgive everyone without exception, without condition, without difference.

Such total forgiveness is not possible for us. The words and the images of our culture are judgmental and condemning. We live in a world which segregates the "criminal" and punishes him. Our daily newspaper concentrates on reporting evil. We call it "news" because we like to read about it; the sins of others help us justify ourselves. We are controlled by law, and the legal terms specify for us whom we shall hate and what we shall punish. In order to forgive, we would have to break away from that whole world and create a new one entirely different.

Exactly. It is not possible for us to find the one perfect "lost chord" on a piano, that calms all troubles and gives perfect peace. But that failure does not lead us to abandon music. If we cannot forgive perfectly we can take the first stumbling steps in that direction. We can rejoice in a growing skill. Jesus came, Paul said, to create all things new and to call us into his new world. We follow him when we strive by forgiving to build his world among us. We can, just as we can make harmony in music.

Early in the public ministry of Jesus, when great crowds gathered around him to hear and be healed, he was in a home in Capernaum. The rooms filled with people, the crowd overflowed into the narrow street. Four men in the city had a friend who was paralyzed, and they decided to bring him to Jesus to be healed. They could not even get close because of the crowd.

Being resourceful men, they took to the flat roofs of the houses. When they had located the room where Jesus was talking, they removed the roof tiles and lowered their friend on his bed with ropes. Jesus did not make a big point of his healing miracles, as though that were the chief thing he had come to do. But neither did he ever refuse a valid request for healing. This challenge, this plea that interrupted his talk to the crowd of people, he accepted just as it was: a request for help.

He looked at the man on the bed and said, "Friend, be happy. Your sins are forgiven." It must have sounded like a cruel comfort to someone who desperately wanted to walk, and nothing else. But Jesus meant it exactly as it sounds, in that context.

Jesus was a self-styled rabbi, a teacher not trained in the official rabbinic schools. So the theologians were present to evaluate him, official students of the Word. They could not let such a statement about forgiveness go unchallenged when it was made by someone outside the establishment. They said, "This is blasphemy. No one can forgive sins except God." But that was not as pious as it sounds. God does not forgive sins directly, and they knew it. They meant, "No one can say that God has forgiven sins except us, his official speakers."

Jesus answered them. He said, in effect, "Why do you immediately turn against someone? Which would be easier for me to say to a paralyzed man, 'Your sins are forgiven' or

ALL SORTS AND CONDITIONS OF SIN

'Take up your bed and walk'? I will prove to you that a man has the power to forgive sins.'' Then he turned to the man on the bed and said, ''Take up your bed and go home.'' The man did. The crowd opened before him, and his friends scrambled to replace the roof tiles and climb down from the roof. Then, Matthew tells us, the crowd glorified God who had given such authority to men!

We can say to anyone the official words, ''Be happy. Your sins are forgiven. They do not stand between you and God.'' We have that authority. It is not limited to the official establishment structures. Jesus has given us a world with such a God. He does forgive sins! We can even go an easier step farther and say the personal words. ''I forgive you all your sins. They do not stand between me and you.'' If we cannot tell a paralyzed man to take up his bed and go home, it is because we are still learning how to say any of the words of forgiveness.

Jesus talked about forgiveness in the Sermon on the Mount, too. He said we should picture ourselves on the way to worship or prayer. Then we remember that someone else has something against us. ''Do not say your prayer or do your worship,'' Jesus said in effect. ''Your first job is to be reconciled to your brother. Then you can pray.''

It is irrelevant to ask whether your brother is right in holding something against you. If he thinks you did something wrong, that's enough. Who started it or who is to blame is unimportant. First you go and forgive him and ask his forgiveness. Then you pray. What you did does not stand between you and God. Your failure to reconcile and be reconciled does. Even if you were right.

We can forgive anything and everyone. In fact, that's the only effective thing we can do. Anything else will fail, even

SEVENTY TIMES SEVEN

worship. We need not bother with the question of who is right and who is wrong. That is meaningless under the universal judgment of God. We can only forgive and be forgiven. When Peter asked how many times, Jesus answered, "Seventy times seven." Translated out of his symbolic idiom, that means, "always, squared and multiplied by ten."

Very few of us are in the helpless state of the paralyzed man that Jesus healed. Our lives are not consumed by sickness, but by jealousy for those who have bested us, anger at those who have wronged us, fear of those who judge and condemn us, hatred of those who threaten us. Jesus would address us in terms a little different from those he used with the helpless man. He would say, no matter what our situation, "Be happy. Their sins are forgiven."

Try this. Take the time to write out a few lists. First list the things others have against you: both what you are and what you have done that needs forgiving for a peaceful fellowship. Write at the bottom of your list, "Be happy. Yours sins are forgiven."

Then make a list of the people you know, with the things they are and do that you must forgive for a peaceful fellowship. You will be surprised at the amount of emotional energy you consume in being against others. Just writing out the list will probably increase your antagonism. So write carefully at the bottom of the list, "Be happy. Theirs sins are forgiven."

Then tell someone—your wife or husband, your friend, your pastor—what you have done and how you feel about it. You need not be specific about what you wrote, but you do need to talk about forgiveness. You are creating a world

ALL SORTS AND CONDITIONS OF SIN

where forgiveness functions, and you do it with words together. No world is made by a person alone, and no communion of people can make one in a single day. But we can forgive, and we can talk about forgiveness. We can make a world of peaceful fellowship together.

As We Forgive Our Debtors

My wife and I ate dinner at a restaurant in St. Louis. The meal was good, the waitress was efficient and friendly, and we enjoyed ourselves. The bill came to $8.75. I gave the waitress a bill, and said, "Keep the change." She accepted it with a smile and walked rapidly to the back of the restaurant, to a door marked Employees Only. And I realized with dismay that the bill I had given her was not a ten, but a twenty.

Naïvely, I spoke to the hostess about it. I wanted to explain that it was a mistake, that I had not really intended such a large tip. She called the waitress and asked. Naturally, the waitress denied my accusation. She took out her bills and said, "See, I don't even have a twenty here!" What could I do? I shrugged it off, and we left. We have not eaten there since, our pleasure spoiled by embarrassment over ten dollars.

I could have spoken to the waitress. I could have said, "I'm sorry you need money. Here's another ten, with my compliments." I am not rich, but I am not poor either. Six months after the loss of ten dollars I would no longer remember it—if I could learn to forgive.

I liked the waitress. She was a cheerful person. She lost my friendship, which probably meant little. She lost her

AS WE FORGIVE OUR DEBTORS

self-esteem, except for the self-justification she probably gained in telling the story of my stupidity. I lost the fellowship of that restaurant in my embarrassment, which I miss. Beside all these losses, the sum of ten dollars is insignificant.

You can do three things with money. You can count it, or you can spend it, or you can use it to make more for you to count or spend. It's very easy to count, and the fact that you can spend it represents the availability of goods and services. Our world has become so thoroughly money-oriented that it is the criterion of our having anything. Most of us, if not in words then in attitudes, make money and security synonymous.

If not in words then in attitudes, money fulfills better than anything else the three-point definition of a god. First, it identifies us in being: I am rich or poor, I make a given salary, I have a certain sum saved, and these things form my image in the minds of those around me. Second, we depend on money for salvation: whatever comes I have insurance, and I am reasonably secure for old age with pensions and savings. Third, money furnishes the criteria of right and wrong: I decide what to do on the basis of its cost or the amount of income it promises.

Perhaps that explains why it is so difficult for us to forgive our money debtors, so hard for us to accept a money loss. The idea of a world where debits and credits are not recorded, where money is given not loaned, where people do not trust savings or insurance appalls us. But money is a false god. It divides us, it sets us against one another. There is no true fellowship in money.

Israel's law of the Jubilee Year was designed to preserve

SEVENTY TIMES SEVEN

fellowship against the divisive effect of wealth. The whole economy was based on ownership of the land. The rules were set up to preserve equality for all time. There could be neither hereditary wealth nor hereditary poverty. Each family was given its plot of land which could never be bought or sold.

Every seventh year the land was to lie fallow. That sabbath year was an act of faith in God. After seven times seven years—the fiftieth year—there was a Year of Jubilee when all debts were forgiven. All land was restored to its original owner, all Israelite slaves were freed. If a man became poor he could sell the use of his land, reckoning the price by the number of years remaining before the Jubilee. Then it would be returned to him. Or he could sell his own services as a slave, the price again being reckoned by the years before the Jubilee when he would again be free. At every fiftieth year the whole people were to be brought back into equality. It was to be a new beginning in all relationships.

It is easy to understand why the law was made. Israel had lived in subjugation in Egypt, where all the land was owned by the Pharaoh (sold for grain under Joseph!). But there is more to the concept than that experience indicates. The covenant of a gracious God made every individual independent. Grace cannot operate well in a culture of class distinctions, of rich and poor, oppressor and oppressed.

There is no record in Jewish history that the Jubilee Year was ever observed. The concept is probably unworkable. It certainly would not work in a money-based economy, with its frequent fluctuations in supply and value of money. It did not work in the land-based economy of Israel, either. The prophets consistently condemn the rich for ignoring the need of the poor. When they called for "justice," they meant economic equality, the material recognition of the validity of every person. Something more than a law returning everyone to land-based equality every fifty years is necessary for the purposes of a covenant of grace.

The purpose of the law of the Jubilee Year is clear: your security is not financial. It rests rather in your relationship with other people. If by our words together we had created a world in which the equal validity of every person is recognized in a material way, we would not need to strive hopelessly for security against others. Without that kind of world our need for security will set us against others.

The concern for personal security is one of the inevitable results of our original sin. The only way we have to determine the adequacy of our material security is comparison with that of others. If we have more than most we feel relatively secure. If we have less than others we fear the future more. It is never enough for us to be rich. We want to be richer than our neighbor; only then can we say we are secure.

One of the mountains we will have to move in order to achieve a world of forgiving is the mountain of money security. Our words of grace together can build a world in which we trust the providence of God rather than our bank account. The first Christian community in Jerusalem expressed that trust in a communal system, where all material goods were regarded as common property. But in the course of years that did not work any better than the law of the Jubilee Year. We do not need a different system; we need a world of trust.

Jesus proposed a means of removing the mountain of our fear for money security; the grace of giving. Giving and

SEVENTY TIMES SEVEN

forgiving are closely allied. Giving is a means for defeating the anxiety that keeps us from forgiving our debtors. Giving reduces the fear that sets us against the thief. The words of giving create a world in which the fellowship of people is more real than money. It is a world in sharp contrast to the one in which the larger public lives. It is a much happier world, but it is very hard to enter. The mountain of the fear for money is immense.

The way Jesus talked about the grace of giving marks the difference between his ethical principle and all others. He said, "Fear not, little flock, for it is your Father's good pleasure to give you the kingdom. Sell your possessions and give alms." Where others have said that you must give or that you should give in order to be good, Jesus said you can. There is no reason for you to be afraid. There is no cause for anxiety. You can even sell all you own and give it all away. Without worry.

If a person steals from you he has not hurt you. He has hurt himself in his relationship to you and to his gracious God. He has perverted his concept of reality in the world and has chosen to make money more real than fellowship. When you fail to forgive him or fail to give (or even, according to the Bible, charge interest on a loan), you do exactly the same thing and suffer the same loss. If a person steals from you, you can without worry simply give him the rest of all you own.

The suggestion troubles us, that we should give to an evil person. In exactly the same way the suggestion that we should forgive an evil person troubles us. But that disturbance is forgetting the universal judgment of God: An evil person is the only kind you can give to. The only kind of person you can forgive is a sinner. There is no other. The

AS WE FORGIVE OUR DEBTORS

money you give is needed by the poor or the thief. But the need to give is in you. The person who has wronged you or the person you dislike needs your forgiveness. But the need to forgive is in you. The giver is the one who profits from giving. The forgiver is the one who is blessed in the forgiving.

You can forgive even the person who steals from you or fails to pay his debts. There is no reason to fear or be anxious.

You can even give away all you own, surrender it all, and remain unhurt. It may be very hard to understand that and even harder to trust it. Yet that is exactly the conviction of those who follow Jesus. The world we create by the words of giving and forgiving is a much happier world. Faith means exactly that we trust our convictional truth and live by it.

Try it. You can start easily at your grocery store or the restaurant or wherever you buy anything. Do not count your change. Try this for the sake of open fellowship with the clerk or the waitress, a fellowship that pays no attention to the question of being cheated. It makes no difference at all. If you are shortchanged, you are not hurt. Only the clerk suffers. You will not help him by checking up on him. You will help him and yourself only by grace, acceptance of the person without concern for sin. Do not count your change. You can forgive.

Try another way that will take a lot longer. Regard yourself as overpaid for your work. Tell yourself and those to whom you talk that you are overpaid. Do not join those who want higher wages. To justify their desire they regard themselves as worth more and their employer as a dishonest person who withholds their honest pay. The justification is irrelevant. In forgiving grace, your employer's honesty or dishonesty makes no difference in your relationship to him. In forgiving grace your relative worth makes no difference in his relationship to you. You can forgive him without loss and without anxiety even if he does underpay you; he can forgive you without loss and without anxiety even if he does overpay you. Mark the irrelevance of the question by saying that you are overpaid. You make your world with words. Make it a world of grace, of the more abundant life in joy, with the words of acceptance. It may take a year or more of saying it to convince you, but you will be a happier person.

Jesus suggested an exercise in giving that sounds simple, but is powerful. He said, "When you give alms, do not let your left hand know what your right hand is doing." Whatever else that means, it means that you do not justify yourself in your giving, that you keep no records. Not even for your income tax returns. That's single-entry bookkeeping. You may remember what you owe to others, but do not remember and do not record what others owe you. Try it at least for part of what you give.

A Good or Bad Reputation

David was never secure on the throne of Israel. In later centuries the people acknowledged that he was a hero and a deliverer, but while he reigned he had to prove himself worthy and powerful to maintain their support. God's people were and still are a fiercely independent people. They had elected David as king, and he ruled only by their consent.

He had sons by several wives. The prospect of power by succession to the throne set these sons against one another; David's family life was not peaceful or happy. Absalom, his third son, plotted to take over the kingdom. He invited David's strongest supporters to a banquet in a city some distance away; and they came, ignorant of his real purpose. While they were out of Jerusalem, Absalom assembled his own supporters and declared himself king. David, taken by surprise without his supporters, had to flee. He left Jerusalem with his court and his immediate bodyguard, and Absalom took over the palace.

David and his men came to Bohurim, where the road ran along beside a hill. Shimei, son of one of the officers of Saul, David's predecessor, met him and vented his anger. He stood on the hill and cursed David for the way he had taken the kingdom from Saul's son. He threw stones and dust at the fleeing court on the road below him, yelling out his accusations.

The scene is comic, and the Bible tells the story well. The mighty king David, his renowned generals and the remnant of his army, trying to maintain dignity while one wild man runs along the hill beside the road throwing stones and calling names. A king cannot stand for that kind of public derision and keep his self-respect as a king. At least, that's what Abishai, one of the generals, thought. He said to David, "Why should this dead dog curse the king? Let me go over and take off his head."

But David said, "Look. My son has taken my kingdom and is trying to kill me. Why should I be troubled by this character? He is only doing what his God tells him he should do. Let him alone. Maybe in the end it will turn out he was right." David and his party went on, and Shimei went home. Absalom was defeated and killed. David returned to Jerusalem in triumph. Shimei came to meet him where he crossed the Jordan River and asked for forgiveness.

Abishai, the law-and-order military mind, again said, "This is the character who threw stones. Everybody knows he did it. Shouldn't he die for it?" David said, "But this is a day to be happy on. No one will die!" And he promised Shimei his life. I try to imagine what Abishai thought of David. That he had damaged his reputation, that he was encouraging disrespect and disloyalty, that he was paving the way for the next rebellion? That he was soft and weak? Probably. But David was not troubled by what Abishai thought. In that respect he was a king and in control.

Concern for a good reputation is one of the mountains we will have to move in order to forgive. It stands in our way.

A GOOD OR BAD REPUTATION

The words of the world around us are not the words of the new world of Jesus Christ. The old world's words define for us what is good and acceptable. In fear of them we fail to use the words of forgiveness. A husband cannot forgive an "unfaithful" wife because the reputation of being bested sexually is unbearable. A wife cannot forgive a wandering husband because she cannot let others think of her as inadequate. Parents must punish rather than forgive their children, or the neighbors will think they have no power to control. An employer cannot forgive an employee because he knows his reputation for discipline is all he has to control others. A church cannot accept a thief or a prostitute because the members know that their influence and acceptability will be destroyed in the community. A business man cannot give to or forgive a panhandler on the street in fear of a reputation as an easy mark. We cannot even forgive such minor things as nagging or chronic lateness or "improper" dress in our friends for fear that our forgiveness will be regarded as approval. If we forgive, we might be marked in public by the failures of our friends.

Our fear of a bad reputation is one of the reasons we stereotype people, identifying a person by the class to which he belongs rather than knowing him as an individual. At one time Protestants had to avoid friendship with Catholics because we regarded Catholicism as a political and religious evil. We segregated blacks because we classified all blacks as dishonest. Smoking and pool halls were forbidden to us because people who smoked were dissolute and gathered in pool halls. We were related to people in the terms of the knowledge of good and evil, and our classification of evil was more important to us than the individual person we classified.

SEVENTY TIMES SEVEN

Many of these stereotypes have been discredited today by compulsory public education and by urbanization. Typecasting did not work when we came into contact with real people. But the fear of a tarnished reputation because of "evil companions" remains with us, and we are still afraid to forgive.

One of the principal methods of protecting our reputation and being "good church members" at the same time is our insistence on repentance and reform before we will forgive. When a thief has demonstrated to the world that he is no longer a thief, we can forgive him. Our acceptance of him will no longer harm us.

The process is psychological nonsense. No person will repent under the pressure of your condemnation. You have to forgive him before he can be sorry for what he did. If you try to make him earn his forgiveness by showing that he is sorry, you will fail. He may do what you ask, but you will not have reconciled him or restored your relationship. You will only have added another blow on the wedge that is driving you apart. Forgiveness is not forgiveness if it must be earned. Sorrow is not sorrow if it is forced on a person.

The only way you can forgive is freely and without any conditions, whether the person you forgive is sorry or not, and certainly before you know that he is sorry. If your anxiety about what people will think keeps you from forgiving openly and freely on your own, then forgiveness will never happen. You have to remember that the "guilty party" is the one that has lost in the act that made him guilty. If someone steals from you, he has lost more than you have. Then the chance to restore is mostly yours, not his. You can forgive, and then he can be sorry.

David was able to forgive Shimei, as he himself said it,

A GOOD OR BAD REPUTATION

because at the time he had no reputation to protect. Before he died, knowing that his power and his name were intact, he instructed Solomon, his son, to do something about the insult he had sustained. So David, in the end, lost the joy of his forgiving.

We can forgive if we remember that we have no reputation to protect. That is exactly what the church has always meant by the phrase "justified by grace." Our excuse for being, the value that justifies our being here at all, is not our own accomplishment but the fact that we are loved. A baby needs no other justification. It is only as we grow older and begin to operate with right and wrong that we feel the need for other justification. "Knowing good and evil" is a Hebrew idiom for growing up.

Jesus told his followers that they should become as little children, justified only by the fact that someone loves them. A child in kindergarten knows that his drawing is good because his mother loves him. As he grows older the rules about good and bad drawing begin to trouble him. He either abandons drawing or makes his own rules about what is good and bad to justify his work or frantically strives to excel in the rules of others. The Word that is Jesus Christ goes back to the basic fact: you neither need nor have any justification except that you are loved. We are justified by grace.

We try for another justification when we try for a good reputation among other people. Our concern for a good reputation is a denial of our faith. So St. Paul wrote to the Christians at Philippi that they should adopt the mind of Christ, who "made himself of no reputation." In its effect on us, a "good reputation" is a danger or even an evil thing. It may ruin our freedom to relate to other people.

SEVENTY TIMES SEVEN

We can't desire a "bad reputation." That would be the other side of an evil coin. We can try to have no reputation at all. We can live in faith, trusting the way of Jesus with no anxiety about what "people will say." We can be known as "easy marks," or "soft touches." We can be known as people who will accept anyone, believe anything. In short, we can forgive.

But not unless we move the mountain of concern for reputation that stands in our way. We do that moving with the words of faith. We talk about forgiveness to create a world where forgiveness is the happy thing to do, where the acts of our associates do not disturb our own self-image. We talk about forgiveness until we realize that the only way we can live openly and unafraid with other people is the way of forgiveness.

Try it. Where you live, where you work, or where you worship, there is a division of life-styles or a clash of opinions on some issue. People do tend to clique, and if there is no real point of division given to us we will make one. Each side of the division will defend its way against the other, with varying degrees of heat. The division may be a political issue, a moral issue, or even something so simple as the way we dress. It need not be important. You are only gaining practice in moving the mountain of reputation.

Do not place yourself on either side of the division. Try to be known as one who accepts both. When you are with people on one side of the issue, defend those on the other side. Use the same smile of greeting with those on either side. When you have practiced a while, tell someone what you have done and how you feel about it. Do not expect instant success. Moving mountains takes time. But the

A GOOD OR BAD REPUTATION

experience may help you forgive even a known public evil, without anxiety about your reputation.

Or try a different experiment on the opposite side of the ledger. Most of us materially alter our character when we are alone behind the wheel of a car. The car is a relatively private place, and in the transient population of the highway we are anonymous. We have no reputation to protect. So we freely vent our anger and express our judgment of other drivers. For a few weeks, try forgiving where there is no question of "what people will say." Relax, understand the other driver's needs, demand no rights of your own, and smile in open friendship no matter what the other driver does. Again, tell someone what you have tried to do, why you did it, and how it made you feel.

Not Ashamed

The hardest sin to forgive today is sexual sin—infidelity in marriage, promiscuity or "perversion." We are generally more anxious about that than about any other sin. When the words of our conversation are the "new morality" or "permissive ethics," the image in our minds is sexual. One of the major reasons for the anxiety is envy. Our society has so exalted the sexual experience that we cannot picture the sexual "sinner" as the loser in his sin. Whenever I have spoken on the subject of morality or ethics to any group, many of the questions asked revealed the envy of the questioners: "Why should others be permitted such freedom when we were or are restricted?"

I dreamed recently that I was at a party of sexual libertines. It was one of those dreams that seem so real it is hard to distinguish between dream and life. The scene was right out of the Playboy *image—wealth and beauty and* savoir faire *on open display. In the dream I was one of the regulars, not a stranger. I felt myself a participant in the life-style of the group. They were my kind of people. It was not just a one-night party. I had the feeling that the action was permanent, that this is the way we lived. We drank and ate and danced to our experience of the "thrills of freedom."*

One man dominated the scene—the life of the party. He

was the leader in our revelry, the man at whose home we gathered, who set the tone for all that happened. He was young and dynamic. In the dream another man confessed to the leader some minor failure. I have forgotten what it was, but it was something unimportant like spilling a drink or being improperly dressed. The leader said, "You will have to run around the track four times for that!"

In the dream the realization came to me that he was serious. It was a punishment he prescribed, and the man who confessed failure would have to do what he was told. There was no freedom there. Conformity was just as important as in any other life-style. The leader was no friend, but a tyrant. In the dream I felt that this man would have to be destroyed. I was lying on the floor, he was sitting on a sofa nearby. I felt a hatchet lying on the floor near me. I rose up, hatchet in hand, and struck a mighty blow at his head.

He disappeared before the blow was struck. Suddenly a profound sense of peace and quiet overwhelmed all who were there. We had been freed from the bonds of frantic thrill that had possessed us all. Everyone there relaxed, and we looked at one another with a new insight into what we were doing. It was such a deep and moving experience of joy at being released that I said, aloud, "Good Lord!" And woke myself up. The feeling of release and joy continued, and I said again, "Good Lord!" Then, realizing that I might wake my wife and be compelled to explain, I muttered again, "Good Lord!"

It was a Saturday night, and I had been asked to preach the next morning on the text of Colossians 3:1-17. I abandoned my notes and told the story of my dream to the church. Paul had written to the Colossians that we should put to death what is earthly in us: immorality, passion, evil desire, covetousness. We should put on as God's chosen ones, compassion, kindness, lowliness, meekness, and patience. "And above all these put on love . . . forgiving each other." These are not rules for a dull and miserable life. They are the prescription of joy, the means to profound peace and happiness.

One Bible paradigm of sexual freedom and love is the Old Testament prophet Hosea. We do not really know his story, because he gives only two small hints of it in his written work. But we can piece them together to make a story on which interpreters generally agree.

Here is the story. In the popular mind of those days, a god went with the land where he was worshiped. If you lived in the land of Dagon, he was your god and you worshiped him. The gods of the land of Canaan were agricultural gods, both male and female. The crops of the land were their fruit, products of their divine copulation. Worship was sexual. A worshiper induced the gods to bear fruit in crops by having sexual intercourse, tempting the gods to follow his example. So every local temple had its prostitutes, who insured a healthy harvest by having intercourse with those who came to worship.

The people of Israel worshiped Yahweh, the God of their covenant. But they came into a land where standard agricultural procedure included intercourse in the temple. They had not been an agricultural people, they had to become one. Many of them saw no difficulty in both worshiping Yahweh and insuring their crops in the standard manner.

Gomer was a temple prostitute. Hosea loved her and

married her. But after a time she tired of marriage or felt called to return to her career, and Hosea was not sure of the parentage of his children. But he loved her still, and in love bought her exclusive services from the temple where she worked. The terms of the service contract were clear: for a set number of days she was to be faithful to him, and he would be faithful to her. His love for her overcame the anxiety of her faithless career.

The experience of his own love is the heart of Hosea's prophecy. Faithless Israel was the bride of God. He had called her and loved her and healed her illnesses. She left God to trust in Egypt and in Assyria and in her own kings and was destroyed. But the love of God does not end. He called her back to faithfulness, forgave her for her harlotry, and promised her renewed joy and prosperity.

This understanding of God's love in spite of Israel's faithlessness did not come to Hosea easily. His own love for Gomer meant social disaster to him. The people of Israel strongly emphasized the purity of genetic lines. They believed that a child was wholly the product of the male seed, the woman only carried it. So Jacob's two wives could each offer her maid to Jacob and call the children that were born their own. The mistress had only commanded her slave to carry her child for a while. But if a woman had intercourse with another male any future child of hers was open to question. She was adulterated. The child of an unfaithful wife could not inherit his father's property. So Israel's whole economy depended on the purity of the line of inheritance, and the commandment against adultery was economically necessary: You shall not call your neighbor's inheritance into question by adulterating his wife.

A man's standing in the community in this family-centered society depended on the fidelity of his wife. When Absalom rebelled against David, his ultimate insult was public intercourse with David's concubines. When David returned to power, he shut those concubines apart and never saw them again. No child that they bore could be proven to be his. No prostitute could ever have a place in any honorable family structure even though she was accepted as a part of the whole society. She could have no share in the land economy, nor could she ever win it.

Against this cultural background we can realize that Hosea's acceptance of Gomer was not a small forgiveness. By it he renounced title to his land for his children, and he was probably ostracized from the honorable family relationships of his village. The social pressures against his forgiving Gomer were more powerful in his day than they would be in ours. Yet he forgave without limit, because he loved. More, he learned in that experience what the love of God is like! He found the joyful, more abundant life.

Nearly all of our fears about sexual sin are caused, or at least conditioned, by the sanctions of the society in which we live. They are made evil by the world we live in, by the words and images of that world's definitions of good and evil. We are hurt by someone else's infidelity only because our social world says we should be hurt. The extent of our hurt is determined by the words and images in which our society has created our world.

The myth of the happy sinner affects us more in our attitude toward sex than in any other problem area of life. The myth is logical and reasonable. Sex experiences are happy. There is great physical pleasure in them. In our culture it is the one pleasure reserved for adulthood. We have made it by our words the symbol of adulthood. By our careful distinction of sex roles, we have made sexual intercourse the proof of manhood for the male, and the proof of meaning in a male-dominated world for the female.

Sex is one of the few instinctive drives that motivate us. It is tied to the instinct for the preservation of the race. Because we have not been able to trust the instincts of parenthood, we have bound sex with a host of rules. We have tried to use sexual desires to insure a stable home life for our children by limiting sex expression to the formal bonds of marriage. We have made so many rules—often rather foolish rules—that the expression of sex has become identified with the normal adolescent rebellion. For the adult it is the symbol of freedom and independence.

All of these words combine to create the image of the happy sexual sinner. When we talk about "the sober and decent life" of the Christian or the "uncontrolled passions of the heathen" the image in our minds is chiefly sexual. The church has achieved the image of a life and joy-destroying force because of its sexual anxieties. When church members talk about "temptation," with the image of something desirable, they imagine primarily sexual "freedom."

St. Paul wrote to the Romans about a natural law, that "when I want to do right, evil lies close at hand." Our sexual rules had a good purpose, the accomplishment has not been good. They have not led us to desire faith and reject sin. The result has been exactly the opposite. We have created by our words a desire for sex and a rejection of the faith. We have led ourselves by our words to deny this life "and all its sordid treasures" and to expect from God a reward for being miserable.

Our fears and our worries about sex spill over into many

other areas. Pornography is with us chiefly because of our oppressive rules; we campaign against it because we are afraid it will increase or falsify our sexual desire. We fight against birth control and abortion because we are afraid they will lead to "sexual license." We are anxious about drugs because in our mental images they are linked with sexual experience. We even descend to racial bigotry for fear of losing in sexual competition. Sex may not be our only reason for these fears, it is certainly one of them.

The weight and the prevalence of our images about sex make it difficult to overcome the myth of the happy sex sinner. But it is as false in the area of sex as it is in any other area. The sex hedonist who moves from experience to experience is not free, nor is he living a joyful life. He is rather searching for a meaning and a purpose where he will not find it—hunting for a needle in a haystack where no needle has been hidden.

We cannot condemn sex experience as an evil in itself. It is not. We need to remove the mountains of sexual fear and envy that stand in the way of forgiving, of a more abundant life. The only method we can follow is the biblical way. Ignoring the irrelevant question of good and evil, we can create together a world of peaceful and accepting relationship between the sexes.

It is easy for us to forgive the polygamy of a distant foreign people. It would be hard to forgive the same thing in a neighbor and even harder in a wife or a husband. The closer you live to someone, the harder it is to forgive him. When you are married to someone, you are forced by social pressure to adapt to him. Then there are hundreds of small and large aggravations driving you apart. They all build up to a trapped feeling, a longing for freedom, a desire for something else. Then the socially conditioned fear and envy of sexual expression is the lighted match above the powder keg, threatening explosion. The partner who wants freedom looks for it in extra-marital sex. The partner who has been "wronged" uses that act as an excuse to dissolve a relationship that he no longer wants to preserve.

Unless we can learn to forgive— The marriage ceremony *does* do more for a couple than give them the right to sue one another. It is a public commitment to the practice of forgiveness. If you want to live that close to someone, you have to learn to forgive and adapt to those hundreds of aggravations. Not merely as a surrender to them, but as the only effective method of correcting them. Marriage is not only the hardest place to forgive, it is also the primary school of forgiveness. It is or can be the place where the joy of the Way of Christ is first and most deeply experienced.

The world we live in is created by the words we use. The words "sexual freedom" make a strange and false world. The image in the word "freedom" is an escape from bondage, a getting out of a slave status. The words force us to see sex as a set of rules, a legal code complete with its prescribed punishment for any infraction of the rules. Because our words make marriage the accepted place for sex, marriage becomes a prison where husband and wife alternate in the roles of prisoner and warden. The image is itself sin because it sets two people against one another. The very words we use to create our world cause the trouble we have living in it.

We will have to change our words and find new images if we want to live in a happy Christian world. The first step toward that change is learning to forgive sexual infidelity as we forgive any other failure. In a Christian world we are not held together by law and punishment. Under the universal judgment of God no one among us can assume the role of warden to prisoner. We are held together by forgiving love and by nothing else. Marriage, like anything else in God's world, is saved by grace and not by law.

Very few marriages are destroyed by sexual infidelity. Except for the power of social pressure created in the words of the world around us, it is no more damaging to a relationship than consuming devotion to a hobby or a hundred other passions we have learned to live with. Usually, the infidelity is caused by the destructive force of law and punishment. The marriage is dissolved by the fear and envy of sexual experience imposed on us by words. Forgiveness means understanding the forces which lead to an act, sympathy with the failure of those involved in the act, a rejection of any concept of punishment, and a desire to reconcile all of the people in the difficulty.

It will work. You can forgive. Your marriage, your love, your security will not be weakened or destroyed. Forgiveness is the only hope you have of restoring or strengthening them. You can forgive: you can't afford not to. Your image among the people you live with will not be weakened or destroyed. Their rules of what is proper need not disturb you if your "right and proper" begins with forgiveness. Forgiving is the strong act, anything else is yielding to others. You can forgive: you can't afford not to.

Two people can learn to love each other *because* they are free to leave at any time. It is the heart of love and the heart of forgiveness.

Try it. Words have bound us, words tear us apart, and words must also function in reconciliation. Even when the

NOT ASHAMED

only person you need to be reconciled to is yourself. You need to talk about this aspect of forgiveness.

If you are married, talk with your marriage partner. Talk as though everything were forgiven, the jealousy and judgment as well as the weakness. If it is too hard to change the climate in the middle of a storm, start talking about other people with words of forgiveness: friends, fellow workers, neighbors, the latest "scandal" in the news.

If you are not married and are not sharing your sexual life with one person, you are in one way or another an important part of the sexual world we create in our words together. When you talk in that world, do it as though you have been forgiven: you have no reason to prove anything, defend anything, or hide anything.

There will be no sudden success or change. We have several centuries of world-building words to overcome on the way. We can do it only if we talk as though all were forgiven; the longing, the loneliness, the disillusionment, the fear, the shame, the love, the peace, the joy.

The Sheep and the Goats

To the people of Palestine, Jesus was a wandering rabbi, a teacher, and nothing more. There were stories about his miracles, but you can't believe everything you hear. Some of the stories that he told in his preaching were repeated, and that was something else. He was an exciting rabbi. He was rapidly gaining a reputation and a following. He was news. So one day he was invited to a dinner party by a man named Simon, an important and wealthy member of the most respected class—a Pharisee.

Some customs change over the centuries, some do not. In those days you greeted guests at your door with a kiss rather than a handshake. Important guests were often given oil for their hair, to cool them. It was a hot country, before the days of air conditioning or shampoo. All the guests had their feet washed as they entered. The streets were not paved, and open sandals were the only footware. They ate their dinner in the Roman style, reclining at a low table rather than sitting. Rome was the ruling power in the world, and then as now influential people adopted the styles of power.

Some other customs have not changed since that day. Jesus was news, but he was not one of the upper class. It was an in thing to invite someone like him to a dinner party—to add interest, to make the affair exciting. But he

THE SHEEP AND THE GOATS

had no political influence, no one important was his friend, few of the people at the party would ever meet him again, he was not socially acceptable in their class. So his feet were not washed when he came, his host did not greet him at the door, he received no treatment for his hair. The basis for his presence there had to be made clear to him. He was welcome as token entertainment, but the host could not be expected to cross class lines or pretend that Jesus was one of his kind.

One of the prostitutes of the city heard that he was at the banquet. She may even have seen him arrive. She crashed the party, not to eat but to show her gratitude for Jesus and his words. She stood at his feet crying. With her hair unbound—a social gaffe—she wiped his feet and poured ointment over them.

The whole event was acutely embarrassing to the dinner party. The woman was not welcome. Jesus was interesting and respectable, but she was not. Everyone there knew what she was. But on the other hand you do not just throw out a person who is honoring a guest at your table. They all felt that Jesus should have quieted her and asked her to leave. It was his responsibility. But he did not. So Simon muttered at the head of the table that if Jesus were all that smart a teacher he would have known what kind of woman she was, and he would have gotten rid of her.

Jesus knew the embarrassment of the people around him. He undoubtedly knew what they expected of him. But he waited until the woman had finished her act of thanks. Then while she waited, he turned to his host and said, "Simon, I have something to say to you." Simon answered, probably with a tone that capitalized and underlined the word of address, "What is it, *Teacher?*" Then Jesus told a story, as

SEVENTY TIMES SEVEN

he often did. "A certain creditor had two debtors. One owed five hundred dollars, the other fifty. He realized that they could not pay him, so he forgave them both. Now, which of the two was most grateful?" Simon in his scorn did not catch the point of the story, but he played along. "Why, I suppose the one who was forgiven most."

"Right," Jesus said. "Now check the difference between you and this woman. You did not have my feet washed. She washed them with her tears. You did not greet me. She has kissed even my feet. You gave me no oil for my hair, but she has given me much more valuable ointment for my feet. Now I will tell you. The woman is a sinner. But she is obviously forgiven because she loves a great deal. When you are not forgiven, you do not love." Then he spoke to the woman, "Your faith has saved you. Go in peace."

Jesus knew who the woman was. He had probably spoken to her before. What she knew of forgiveness she had learned from him. She knew that he would accept her when she crashed Simon's party. Simon also knew who she was. He had talked about her if not to her before this. She was grateful for forgiveness from Jesus because of the treatment she received from Simon. She knew before she crashed his party that he would not accept her or welcome her.

It is irrelevant to indentify Simon as a Pharisee or the woman as a prostitute. That is stereotyping. He was a person, and she was a person. The whole point of Jesus' presence at the banquet and his treatment of the woman was that there was no difference between Simon and her. He accepted them both alike. He was not troubled by Simon's lack of courtesy, and he was not troubled by the woman's act of gratitude. He was not even troubled by the silent embarrassment of the rest of the dinner party.

THE SHEEP AND THE GOATS

The woman and the man would have agreed on several points. First, there are certain things you cannot do and remain good in the eyes of other people. Second, she did them, he did not. Third, therefore he was a better person than she was. But all of these points were established in their world by the words they spoke and the images they agreed on in those words. Jesus quite specifically denied that world. He made a new one for us with the words of forgiveness. First, we are not made good by our keeping of the law, but by our relationship to one another in forgiveness and love. Second, she met forgiveness, accepted it, and was willing to forgive. Third, she was given righteousness in the new world of Jesus Christ, he was not even in that world.

There is no difference in sin between people. But we cannot pretend that we are all alike in relationship to Jesus Christ. As long as Simon continued in his way of refusing to be forgiven and to forgive, he would be excluded from the fellowship of Jesus and the woman. Not as punishment, but because he was creating a different world to live in. His world of words shaped him in a different pattern of self-image and character. Sooner or later he would have to be told that his world was different. Jesus would even have to tell both his followers and Simon's friends that their worlds were different and that they had no fellowship.

Simon assumed the power to judge and condemn the woman who crashed his dinner party. We have assumed the same power. Simon was amazed that Jesus did not join him in his condemnation. We take it for granted that Jesus joins in ours. We have even twisted the words of Jesus giving us power to forgive, to make them sound as though we have power to decide who shall be condemned as a sinner. Simon felt justified in condemning the woman because she had obviously broken an absolute law. We justify ourselves in the same way, talking profoundly about the absolute law of God. But in Simon's act of judgment as in ours, the "absolute" law becomes relative, one used to separate ourselves from a sinner.

There are absolute laws which are valid always and in every place. But only God can make or administer an absolute law. The moment any human being attempts to apply that law to another human being it becomes relative. It is conditioned by his understanding and interpretation of both law and event, and that understanding is colored by his need to justify himself in the terms of good and evil.

We do not have the power to adjudicate by law, with condemnation and punishment, in the kingdom of heaven. It has not been given to us, even though the church has assumed it. The only power that has been given to us is the power to forgive. With that power alone we discipline ourselves and "mark those who cause divisions and offences" among us. If our brother trespasses against us we are sent to him with words of forgiveness. If he hears us and joins us in our trust, we have gained him. If he does not hear and rejects forgiveness, we may bring others along to speak forgiveness. If he does not listen to them or to the whole church, we regard him as an outsider, one who does not belong to our world.

But we do not ever stop forgiving. That is our ministry. When we forgive someone he is forgiven. If we do not forgive, there is no one else who will, and he is not forgiven. We cannot decide in advance which sinners we will accept; we accept and forgive them all. We even forgive the man who does not know himself as a sinner and

THE SHEEP AND THE GOATS

rejects our forgiveness. Our discipline does not ever remove a person from our physical presence or deny him the hearing of the words of grace.

The kingdom of heaven comes among us when we talk the language of forgiveness. If we are to create that new world among us, then it must be the language of forgiveness that we talk. We must mark one who speaks the words of judgment and condemnation as belonging to a different world, but we do not punish him or exclude him from our forgiveness. By our words and by our actions we tell him that he lives in a different world. We invite him to the kingdom of heaven with forgiveness, always, squared and multiplied by ten.

Try it. Listen to the words of your friends, also in the church, when they talk about other people. Listen particularly to your own words. Wherever you hear the words of forgiveness, join that talk. Ask about it, evaluate it, feel it. If you hear no words of forgiveness, do not condemn but speak them yourself. When the people to whom you talk ask you about forgiveness, tell them about your own. And be happy, you are forgiven.

The Yoke of Falsehood

Jeremiah lived and taught in the last days of the kingdom of Judah. He had seen a vision, and he said that he had been called by God to speak the words of God. He was not the only prophet around. Since the days of David, prophets had been appointed by the king, their office was a state function. So there were some four hundred state prophets who opposed Jeremiah and said he lied. A man named Hananiah was the leader of these official prophets.

The armies of Babylon had already conquered Jerusalem. They had taken Jeconiah the king and most of the important leaders to Babylon in exile, and they had put Zedekiah on the throne in Jerusalem. Zedekiah listened to his official prophets and believed that the covenant and the temple put God on their side as a nation, and he rebelled against Babylon. The Babylonian armies came back, surrounded the city of Jerusalem, and cut off all supplies.

Jeremiah made a yoke of wood, like the ones oxen wear to pull a heavy load. He put it on his shoulders as an object lesson to convince the people. He went to the temple courtyard, assembly place for all major events. The people gathered around to see what it meant that a prophet stood among them wearing a wooden yoke. Jeremiah said, "Bring your necks under the yoke of the king of Babylon

THE YOKE OF FALSEHOOD

and serve him and his people and live. Why should you die by the sword, by famine, and by pestilence? Do not listen to the prophets who tell you that you shall not serve the king of Babylon! They are telling you a lie!''

Now, Jerusalem was at war. In a time of war you cannot permit a man like Jeremiah to undermine the spirit of the people, to threaten national security. Jeremiah had to be silenced. Hananiah came out of his office, followed by the assistant prophets. He took the yoke from the neck of Jeremiah and broke it. He said, "Thus says the Lord of hosts, the God of Israel, 'I have broken the yoke of the king of Babylon. Within two years I will bring back to Jerusalem all that has already been taken.'"

It was not enough. Somehow Jeremiah had to be discredited. So his enemies denounced him as a traitor and a heretic. They framed him on a charge of desertion to the enemy, and they threw him into prison. They starved him on bread and water, and they threw him into an unused cistern up to his knees in mud. He was finally rescued by a Gentile in the court, who did not feel threatened by his words.

Zedekiah suspected that Jeremiah was right. But he did not know. Both sides said, "Thus says the Lord!" It was a theological controversy with one prophet against four hundred. All of them were sincere. All of them believed. The true prophet knows that he has been called by God, but the false prophet does not know that he has not been called. So each side said the other lied, Zedekiah and his people had to choose.

Well, they made a majority decision and followed Hananiah. Having chosen, they truly believed that they were right. But they were wrong; Jeremiah was right.

SEVENTY TIMES SEVEN

Jerusalem was destroyed, the temple torn to the ground. The people were deported to Babylon for seventy years of exile.

There have been "false teachers" among us in every generation since the time of Jesus Christ. Men have risen up within the church to say that what the official teachers taught was false. They have been denounced as traitors and heretics. In times and places that the church has had the power, it has fallen into terrible error by torturing and killing them. It has always seemed the right thing to do.

We have our heretics today, as in every generation. In nearly every communion of the church, there are men who are being denounced as false teachers who are destroying the faith that has been delivered to us. These are not light and unimportant accusations. The men accused are, in the images of the people, threatening the very world in which we live.

We also have our official prophets today. They are ordained by the church and called to local congregations to speak for God. Their training, their ordination, and their official call place on them the heavy temptation to regard their own words as truth. But they guarantee nothing. I too have had the name and the office of pastor, and I can look back at my ministry appalled by the things I have said in the name of my God. Every pastor who honestly learns as he works learns this also: that he has made mistakes and that he is not protected from error.

We cannot afford to silence the false teacher among us or forbid him to teach. Because we have no other kind of teacher. Our God is a hidden God. He has commanded us to make no image of him because we will inevitably begin to worship that image and cease to learn anything more of his truth. No man knows God enough to fix truth in an image

THE YOKE OF FALSEHOOD

that will always be true. Therefore every man is false in his teaching; the difference in teachers is only a difference in the degree of falseness. When two teachers disagree, they cannot both be right. But that does not mean that one is right and the other wrong. They can both be wrong. The acknowledgment of that weakness is the necessary first step toward the kingdom of heaven, the world of forgiveness. Neither any man among us nor all of us put together can pretend to know enough to forbid any teacher to teach or to punish him in any way for his teaching.

Each of us is a teacher, because each of us has his own conviction of the truth to share. But when Jesus delivered his final speech against those who presumed authority in their teaching, he said, "You are not to be called rabbi, for you have one teacher, and you are all brethren. Neither be called masters, for you have one master, the Christ." Each of us is a teacher, but no one among us has the authority to impose his convictions on any others. We can only share them to create a world together. We teach one another only as equals, sharing our weakness in order to learn about our hidden God.

We teach without authority and without power of our own. We have no weapon against falsehood except our own conviction of the truth. In the world of the words of Jesus Christ, the person who presumes to silence others is wrong for that very reason. We do not even oppose what power we have against his; we can only confess our faith as though he had no power or authority over us. Everything else will fail. In the world of the words of Jesus we know no other authority. Jesus Christ is Lord.

A heretic is not one who teaches falsehood. If that were our definition then all of us would be in some degree heretics. A heretic is one who tries to gain a following for his particular image of God, who constrains others by force or reason to conform to his concepts. We cannot say that every faith is as good as any other, or that it makes no difference what you believe. Some of the worlds built by a teacher's words are unhappy worlds, with gods who are not the Father of our Lord Jesus Christ. We cannot silence these teachers, but we can measure what they say and decide in Jesus Christ not to hear or to follow them. The criterion of measurement was given to us by Jesus, when he warned against the false teachers that would surely come. "By their fruits you shall know them," he said, just as you know whether an apple tree is good or bad.

The Holy Spirit, the spirit of love and forgiveness among us calls us into truth. We have no other guarantor. If we try to guarantee the truth in our own wisdom we have made ourselves competitors of God. We can teach one another how to love and forgive, but if we are to teach that we cannot forbid any man to teach.

Try it. Somewhere in your city or near it, now or in the near future, there will be a political contest. Two or more people will be competing for the same public office. The practice of equal time in the mass media provides you with a cue. Listen to both sides in the contest as though the contestants were teachers. Then examine your own response. Where are your opinions formed? By the speakers on the television or in the newspapers or in your own discussions with your friends? Would your world be a happier one if only one political party were permitted to teach? Would you be flattered or insulted if your employer instructed you to listen to only one of the contestants?

Capital Forgiveness

Few people can talk about death from personal experience. Some of us have watched a person die or have been so close to death that they know its nature. But none of us has been there himself. It is the one place from which you do not return. Death is irreversible and inevitable. We cannot talk about death itself. We can only talk about the effect of that inevitability on the life we live now.

The words are harder to say in the developed nations of the twentieth century than they have been in any other time or place. We are fighting against death, not just as individuals but as a whole culture. We are far from winning the war, but we have won a good number of skirmishes—at least enough to give us hope. People who lived a century or two ago, like those who live now in the poor nations of the world, were much more familiar with death than we are. Parents expected no more than half of their babies to grow to adulthood. Serious illness or accident naturally ended in death. Death hovered in the atmosphere around them in "the good old days," and they treated it much more casually than we can today.

Here and now the same illness or accident that meant death in the past only causes us to rally the immense forces of modern medicine to "save a life." That has become our ultimate ethic, our most sacred cause. We talk about "respect for life" as the one unquestionable good. We regard the man who talks about death casually with suspicion, as though his talk were some form of sacrilege. We launch crusades for the "unalienable rights of the unborn," we argue about the right to die with dignity for the aged, we pay morticians well for their skill in hiding the appearance of death—because our ultimate ethic requires us to extend a physical life as long as possible.

I am conscious of the fact that I have not been touched by death. I talk about it with very few personal experiences to condition my words. The first funeral I ever attended was that of a college professor, where I was a pallbearer. The second came when I was working as pastoral intern in New York, and I was the officiating clergy. The only time that sorrow has been part of my attitude was when I stood alone at the graveside of my stillborn first son and formally repeated the burial liturgy. My words about death cannot carry the weight of experience that others who talk with me have had.

I am dying. I will die. You are dying. You will die. So will everyone else. No one has yet "saved a life." At the best we have only postponed death. I do not know whether that postponement has ever benefited us. Our efforts to postpone death have certainly increased our anxieties and added to the burdens with which we live. I am not about to reject the services of physicians and surgeons. I want to live, as any living thing does. But I also know that I have no respect for life until I have fully adapted by words and images to the fact that I am dying and I will die, and so will everyone else. A world that denies death cannot be a happy world because death is there for all of us.

CAPITAL FORGIVENESS

If we were to accomplish unending life, or even unending youth and vigor, our problems would be so horrendously magnified that we could not cope with them. Try for a moment to imagine what attitudes and practices we would have to change if no one died—or even worse, if it were possible to buy unending life. The accomplishment would increase our bitterness and envy, our meaninglessness, and our loneliness. As we are now, death is not a curse, however much we hate it. Death is a necessary and a blessed component of life. It is not death in itself that destroys life, but the fear of death.

We hate and fear death because of our sense of self-importance. There are tasks we must complete. There are experiences we have not yet had. Tomorrow will be better than today only if we can experience that better tomorrow. The future will provide the meaning that today has not given us. Tomorrow we will succeed. We may yet be known in the world if only we can have tomorrow in which to try. We hate and fear death because it is the denial of such hope, it decides our unimportance. We feel we have no meaning if the meaning cannot be made to last. Permanence has become the primary criterion of good.

No one is that important. The world does not need anyone's tomorrow, and no tomorrow will ever satisfy anyone who is unhappy with today. A happy life is one that may end now. The *only* happy life is one that may end now. To the extent that we need tomorrow to fulfill today, we make today unhappy. The more abundant life of the kingdom of heaven for which we yearn must be now so fulfilled that tomorrow is not necessary. We cannot be happy if tomorrow is essential to our happiness. We cannot say that our world is well created unless we have made it

SEVENTY TIMES SEVEN

and ourselves in it complete enough to have it end today.

The Christian faith, like every other religious faith, promises a different and a better tomorrow after death. The promise is a way to alleviate the fear of death. It gives the hope that the meaning and success we have failed to find today will be there for us in another life. But we have spoiled that hope with the same perverse skill that we spoil all others. We have used the promise of life after death in order to subdue the hopes of oppressed people in this life. We have spent more time and energy describing the eternal death that awaits those who disagree with us than we have spent talking about the hope of life we have. By these means we have increased rather than decreased the fear of death. And very often our description of the other life for which we hope has been so bound by the concepts of this life that it is appalling rather than appealing.

The promise of a life after death was never intended to replace a promise for this one. In fact, meaning and joy in the next life are almost always directly related, in the words of Jesus and his followers, to meaning and joy now. The promise is given to us in order to increase, not decrease, our appreciation of what we have. If we are to create a new world in Jesus Christ by our words and their images, we need to create it for now. We do not know what any future life may be, nor how we shall fit into it. We do know that it is promised in grace, that we do not earn it by suffering and deprivation. We grow into it in the experience of loving and forgiving. We need not try to prolong or replace this life. We need only to enrich it with the coming of the kingdom of heaven, and the future will be cared for.

Our words of forgiveness will adapt to that truth. The man who kills has already lost more in his act than he has

CAPITAL FORGIVENESS

taken from his victim. A life that comes to an abrupt and untimely end is not lost, but a life ruined by a climactic act against another life is. That is the truth which the world we create must contain in order to be a blessed world. It is eminently possible for a follower of Jesus to forgive a killer in sympathy for his loss. That is the only effective deterrent to the act of killing. It can be taught only with the language of forgiveness.

Punishment for the act of killing, particularly capital punishment, teaches exactly the opposite. Extreme punishment for an act requires an extreme effort by the actor to justify his act. The cold violence of capital punishment (or even life imprisonment) provides that justification. The man who contemplates a murder is taught by the threat of punishment that his contemplated act has some validity. The way out of an intolerable situation is the way of extreme jeopardy. The threat teaches me that if I kill and am not caught I will be better off for my act. Just as it teaches me that if I kill one who has killed, or applaud the judge who must, I will be better off.

Jesus, on the way to the cross on Calvary, was a weak and sorry figure. He was emotionally exhausted by the weeks of anticipation, worn out by the last few days of forcing the issue of his own fate. He had been imprisoned, mocked, brutally flogged, and beaten. He was too weak to carry his own cross, which was customary. The soldiers detailed for the execution forced another man to carry it for him. In the crowd that followed them to Calvary were a number of women, weeping in sorrow that such a good man should be brought so low.

Jesus turned to talk to them. I picture it happening at a sudden wide place—perhaps a crossroad—in the narrow street. The entire procession stopped without question while he spoke. The soldiers anxious to finish the job, the other two criminals carrying their own crosses and tasting despair, the officials who had accused Jesus justifying themselves by seeing to it that the sentence was carried out, the crowd of curious people, all stopped and listened. In one way or another they had all been part of the condemnation, but they listened to the condemned.

He said, in effect, "Daughters of Jerusalem, do not cry for me. I am not losing anything. My life has been full like a green tree, and I do not need tomorrow. But weep for yourselves. The time is coming when your life will be unbearable and you will want to die." Then he turned to continue the march, and the whole procession moved with him. They took him out and crucified him with the two thieves. It was a legal execution, as easy to justify as any other act of capital punishment, and Jesus understood. He said, "Father, forgive them. They don't realize what they are doing." He did not mean that his death was a crime greater than any other. He prayed as a man wholly open to the grace of a forgiving God, forgiving his killers.

If we are to create a world where forgiveness works, there can be no end to our words of forgiveness. We forgive those who take our lives, as we forgive any lesser act. We forgive those who place our lives in jeopardy. We forgive those who kill our loved ones, knowing that nothing less than forgiveness will ever effectively alter the pattern of killing. We forgive even those who kill without thought or need, knowing that the killer has lost far more than his victim can. A life that is cut short is not lost, no matter how short it has been. But a life touched by the ultimate act of killing has indeed been lost.

CAPITAL FORGIVENESS

The man who kills does not need our punishment. He needs instead our sympathetic forgiveness. On the other hand, the judge who must sentence the killer to death or prison because of the law of the land does not need our approval. He needs our sympathetic forgiveness, exactly the same as the man he condemns. No other evil in life can equal the damage done by our failure to forgive. No other remedy in life can equal the deterrent effectiveness of forgiveness.

The moral rule (or the command of God) that we shall not kill has always been ambivalent in a time of war. Then we send our representatives or go ourselves for the express purpose of killing—or even worse, maiming—as many as possible. Having condoned that major act, we find ourselves condoning a whole host of lesser acts against people: prostitution, rape, theft, and propaganda untruths. Only one rule is strengthened in war, the rule that we should obey authority. We strengthen that because it provides the structure of official right which justifies all other acts. We cannot permit desertion from the war or grant amnesty to the deserter because we would lose our own justification for killing and raping if we did.

The act of killing is no different in war from what it is in peace. But for our own justification we must create a world in which there is a difference between the two. We do it with the words of military authority and honor. With each succeeding war, the world of war grows farther from the moral world of peace; the justification grows more difficult and the demand for obedience to authority grows more stringent. We need to justify not merely death "by the sword" but more and more sophisticated weapons of cold impersonal killing.

SEVENTY TIMES SEVEN

In the world we create to justify war, the military leaders are given and assume immense power. We are unable to question that power or object to it because we have not learned to forgive. If we could learn to forgive the killer in time of peace, as an effective means of deterrent against killing, we would not need to surrender our honor and freedom to military power in order to justify war. The commanding generals of an army do not need our respect and approval. They need our forgiveness. In a blessed world created by the words of Jesus, they would rejoice in that forgiveness.

It would of course be useless for me to propose the method of forgiveness to the powers of the state for their use. In the world constructed by the words and images of those powers it sounds ridiculous. I am conscious of the folly as I write about it. To the extent that I live in the world built around the relationships of the knowledge of good and evil, I know my words are ridiculous. No judge or jury, having determined the guilt of a murderer, can forgive him. No general or admiral, having determined the necessity of a killing war, can forgive the disobedient. That would be nonsense in our common human world.

I do not intend the proposal to make sense in that common world. Jesus did not live and work among us in order to make a few bad men a little better. He proclaimed the universal judgment of God which recognizes no difference in sin between the killer and his judge; between the general, the deserter, and the enemy. He came to make all things new, to create a new world of grace in which forgiveness can and does function. We who follow Jesus are not called to stop one killing hand, nor to stay one or two sentences from execution within the world of men. We are

CAPITAL FORGIVENESS

called to the much more extreme act of creating a new world as an alternate to the one which has already failed and will fail. We are called to create a world of grace and forgiveness.

We can create that world, as followers of our Lord Jesus Christ. Few among us will ever be called on to forgive one who tries to kill us or one who has killed a friend. But we can use the words of forgiveness in every lesser case, and we can talk about forgiveness until even that ultimate forgiving is reasonable and possible in our world. We may not influence the larger world to abandon war and killing, but we can create an alternate world in which we live by faith, as an example of what the peace of God in Christ can mean. Unless we do, the world of men has no hope.

Epilogue: Happily Ever After

After a week-long workshop in a strange city, I had a Sunday morning free. I decided to attend an inner-city church where a friend was the pastor. I found the church in a semiresidential, changing neighborhood. It was old and beautiful. It was built right up to the sidewalk in front, and close to the houses on either side, in the style of the preautomobile city.

The service was well attended. I felt right at home. The members were my kind of people, the hymns and the prayers were familiar. After the service was over we walked out into a beautiful spring day, the kind that nearly forces you to stand and talk. I was a stranger, so I merely stood and watched the other worshipers. A clean, satisfied, and healthy crowd on a dirty, discouraged, and nearly beaten street.

While I watched, a man who lived in the neighborhood walked past. He was poverty thin, he needed a shave, he was dressed in an old T-shirt and an unpressed suit jacket. He threaded his way through the crowded sidewalk, with exaggerated care not to touch any of the church members.

No one said a word to him, and he made no sound. Most of the people on the sidewalk did not even notice him. I was close to laughter as I watched the two worlds intersect for

EPILOGUE: HAPPILY EVER AFTER

more than a minute. The man whom the worshipers would call a "local bum" seemed to be avoiding contamination from the furs and the well-pressed suits of the followers of Jesus, who was known in his day as the friend of prostitutes and the oppressed..

Across the street another world watched with me: the families of those who lived there sat on their front steps, wholly removed from both the church and the man who slid unrecognized through it. I said nothing, and I did nothing. I was just as clean and well pressed as anyone there. I had placed myself in one world, and the other world was, for that time, beyond my reach.

I am aware of the fact that this world carries a heavy burden of pain, and that I seem to be passing by on the other side with my proposal for the church. Millions are dying in hunger and disease. Isn't it our task as followers of Jesus to feed and heal? Thousands are twisted and stunted under the torture of tyranny. Isn't it our work as followers of Jesus to free the prisoners and oppose the tyrant? Whole nations are breaking under the conflicts of race and class. Shouldn't we as Christians be moving courts and legislatures to justice for all?

Yes.

But telling church members that they should do these things is almost useless. The act of faith is not performed out of a sense of duty, or it is diminished as an act of faith. It is not possible to move an entire church organization even to such an obvious good as the alleviation of hunger in the world, unless every member of the organization is convinced that the move is good. We do not have that conviction. We have gathered into one body all sorts and conditions of men. We have unified them in a confession of faith and the practice of ritual. We have not united ourselves in our will to free prisoners or oppose discrimination. For every voice among us that opposes war there is another voice proposing war as the only alternative to slavery. For every challenge to social action there is an opposition. We speak with a divided voice, and we act with a divided will.

We are not deaf to the call for action. It is the glory of the church that most of those who lead us toward justice and equality have come out of the church. They have heard the stories of Jsus, and they follow him. But again and again they find that their church does not follow them. Leadership is born in the church, but almost inevitably it must lead out of the church. We need the leadership, but we have a greater need for Christians who will follow. When the whole body has learned to talk the language of forgiveness there will be more leaders to move the world; but the world will move only when the church hears its leaders and follows them.

I am aware of the church's present guilt in the malfunctioning of society: loss of hope among the young and the aged, the increasing distance between those who have and those who have not, the polarizing splits between social and governmental philosophies, the vast numbers of lonely and frightened people crushed or torn in struggles over which they have no control. Shouldn't we as Christians propose plans for the healing of society, rather than plans to recreate our own small subculture? We are already a narrow middle stratum of contented people clinging to our contentment. Isn't it our task to break the bonds of satisfaction and share the burdens of the suffering?

Yes.

But we will not do the work because we ought to. There

EPILOGUE: HAPPILY EVER AFTER

are too many broken links in the chains of obligation. We can escape too easily. We will do the work only when we want to. Before that happens both we and our image of the world will have to be remade. We do not need new laws and new challenges. Consciousness of the world's need is already sharp in the church. We do need the words and the experiences that will free us to accept the challenge without anxiety. We need to learn that we want to follow Christ.

I am aware of the power in new movements both inside and outside the church: human development programs, charismatic revivals, effectiveness training, and transactional analysis. Isn't it the work of those who name themselves Christian to follow Jesus in affirming the power of people, in blessing the love God has given wherever it appears?

Yes.

No one successfully builds a tower without carefully laying a foundation. The programs of hope around us will prosper more and live longer if there is a world of people to support them. We need the words and the experiences that will help us understand the hope that is in us all. We also need an alternate world free enough to accept the movement of human growth.

The burden of creating the kingdom of heaven is on the church. We have the words of forgiveness. We have been called to reconcile men: to one another and in that to God. We are not now doing our job. Our record in creating a new world for all sorts and conditions of men is appalling. The inner city is only one of the many witnesses to our failure.

The reasons for our failure lie in our social psyche, our united self-image. We have framed our identity like a photograph and hung it for our own admiration. We stand firm and unmoved, satisfying ourselves with words and images that have no meaning except in our closed circle. We have kept the sacred forms and lost the Spirit, the Holy Mood of the people of God. We need now to shake the present until the forms crack and the Spirit is free.

I would not dare to prescribe the structures of the future. That's the Spirit's work. But I can demonstrate the method with words. If we could shatter the images which now bind our favorite words, we might be able to use them again to build something new.

The *church* is not the good people who are members of an organization, who attend the Sunday morning "worship," and support the work of the organization. The church is all the people who have been given the words of forgiving grace and feel themselves called to practice that grace: to act in faith.

Faith is not believing that the stories of the Bible and the doctrines of the church are true. Faith may doubt all that. Faith is believing that the way of life proposed by the stories and the doctrines is good. Faith is trusting the promise of Jesus and practicing the Way.

Worship is not assembling on Sunday morning to sing some hymns and hear some person preach. Worship may have to reject all that. Worship is all that you do because you are glad God is what Jesus talked about. It is the dance of joy when you have found out that the way of forgiving grace is good.

The *means of grace* are not the words of the Bible and the ritual of the sacraments. Those things may even stunt grace. The means of grace are the words that make us gracious: the stories of what God has done in his people and the memory of Jesus Christ.

EPILOGUE: HAPPILY EVER AFTER

Bible stories are not pious tales with a moral for the children. Most of them can be heard only by adults. Bible stories are our identity as a people. They unite us in the record of our relationship to God. We are those through whose stumbling lurch God has walked in grace among men.

The preacher—or pastor or rector or priest—is not a God-ordained mediator. Each of us is that to all the others. The preacher is a storyteller. He is one who knows the record of what God has done and builds us up with the narration. Over and over again.

The primary job of *church officers* is not to keep order and discipline members. It is decidedly not to maintain the property. They can give that away if they want to, and lose very little. Their primary job is to structure the church program around talk about God in his grace. Call that Christian education. The potluck dinner has always been one of the most honored methods.

Church work is not committee meetings and "socials." They only prepare for the work. Most church work is not even done on the church property. It is feeding the hungry, visiting the lonely, freeing the prisoner, and forgiving the sinner.

We create one another. There is no place where the words of forgiveness and acceptance are not needed. If the words where you work or play with other people are bigoted, harsh, and judgmental, then the world you work in is that way. You can change it. If the words where you work or play are indifferent, self-centered, and cold, then the world you work or play in is that way too. You can change it. Not in a day or a week, perhaps not in years. But change is

SEVENTY TIMES SEVEN

possible, a new world of forgiveness and happiness about people can be created.

You do not need a reputation for faith and love and forgiveness at your church. It should be taken for granted there. But you do need it out where you meet the larger world that men have created. It will not earn anything for you, except possibly some derision for a while. And of course the peace that surpasses understanding: knowing, because you can forgive, that you are forgiven.